The Complete Poems of WILLIAM SHAKESPEARE

And Selected Verse from the Plays

Illustrated

Compiled by George Gesner

AVENEL BOOKS
NEW YORK

Copyright © 1982 by Crown Publishers, Inc.

This 1982 edition is published by Avenel Books, distributed by Crown Publishers, Inc.

Manufactured in the United States of America

Library of Congress Cataloging in Publication Data
Shakespeare, William, 1564–1616.
The complete poems of William Shakespeare and selected verse from his plays.
I. Gesner, George, 1954– . II. Title.
PR2841.G47 1982   821'.3   82-11450
ISBN: 0-517-385651

h g f e d c b a

CONTENTS

FOREWORD

It happens only rarely that an individual distinguishes himself enough to be able to exert influence over the lives of others; it happens even less often that he is able to inspire love. William Shakespeare has done both. He is generally considered the greatest writer to have emerged in English literature. His poetry and plays are the treasures of our language. Many familiar quotations used today, even in informal speech, are Shakespeare's, and it is a fitting tribute to the man, the artist, and the legend.

The Complete Poems of William Shakespeare contains the entire poetic works from his early narrative poems to verse excerpts from the dramas of his later years. This is the standard by which we measure literary excellence. He wrote for our edification, entertainment, and enjoyment.

Very little is known about Shakespeare's life. He was born in 1564 in Stratford-on-Avon and moved to London in the late 1580s to pursue a career in the theatre. He set out to establish himself as a serious poet when he published his erotic narrative treatment of *Venus and Adonis* in 1593. The following year he published *Lucrece*, a serious attempt to deal with tragedy, foreshadowing his later dramas.

There are records of his plays being performed as early 1594 by the Lord Chamberlain's Company, later known as the King's Men when, in 1603, they were taken under the direct patronage of King James. Shakespeare's association with this troupe continued for the rest of his life.

In 1599 his poetry was included in a volume called *The Passionate Pilgrim,* and ten years later his collection of 154 sonnets was published by Thomas Thorpe, apparently without the author's permission. Scholars have determined that these poems were written over a period of five years beginning in 1592. At the time of his death in 1616, half of his plays had never been published. They were finally printed by two of his colleagues at the Globe Theatre, Condell and Heminge, in 1623 in the "First Folio."

Shakespeare spent many years as an actor, but almost no biographical data exists. We are left with the deeds to various pieces of real estate that he owned, a draft of his will, and the rumor that he died a wealthy and contented man. Perhaps this lack of information adds to the intrigue of the poet whose life will probably remain an eternal enigma.

It is in his sequence of 154 sonnets that would-be investigators of Shakespeare's life attempt to construct part of his biography. Sonnets 1 through 126 are addressed to an aristocratic young man and are concerned with the idealized friendship between the poet and the youth. Numbers 127 through 152 deal with the poet's passionate love/hatred for the famous and, incidentally, unidentified dark lady. The sonnets are a collection of lyric poetry that express the psychological state and mood of the poet. However, there is no conclusive evidence to prove that these poems are autobiographical. The sonnets are concerned with such issues as love and lust, guilt and innocence, the recognition and frustration of the temporal bounds of life, and the value of truth and faithfulness to oneself. They are generally thought to be among the finest poetry ever written.

The verse selected from the plays merits attention on its

own. Shakespeare's delight in the diversity of human nature, his willingness to sing for the pain as well as the happiness and truth, his preoccupation with wit and word games and, paradoxically, his naturalness and simplicity are nowhere more evident than in the plays.

The poems are of a wide variety, from the celebrations of *A Midsummer Night's Dream* and the cynicism of Jaques in his "Seven Ages of Man" speech in *As You Like It,* to the tenderness of *Romeo and Juliet* and the dignity of the young Hamlet as he addresses his famous question, "To be or not to be . . ." The credibility of the characters is evidence of Shakespeare's inspiration and genius. Readers must remind themselves that it is the playwright/poet and not the character who is telling the story. And as a teller of stories, a spinner of tales, a re-creator of history, Shakespeare is beyond categorization. His is the voice that speaks clearly across the centuries. As an Elizabethan who wrote for himself and his contemporaries, his creative energy and intellectual curiosity have not been affected by the passage of time. His plays are equally as significant in the modern world as they were in his own. *The Complete Poems of William Shakespeare* is a collection of his treasured works to be enjoyed as they have been for the past four centuries.

JULIE MARS

Venus and Adonis

TO THE

RIGHT HONOURABLE
HENRY WRIOTHESLY,
EARL OF SOUTHAMPTON,
AND BARON OF TICHFIELD

RIGHT HONOURABLE,

I know not how I shall offend in dedicating my un-polished lines to your lordship, nor how the world will cen-sure me for choosing so strong a prop to support so weak a burden: only, if your honour seem but pleased, I account myself highly praised, and vow to take advantage of all idle hours, till I have honoured you with some graver labour. But if the first heir of my invention prove deformed, I shall be sorry it had so noble a god-father, and never after ear so barren a land, for fear it yield me still so bad a harvest. I leave it to your honourable survey, and your honour to your heart's content; which I wish may always answer your own wish, and the world's hopeful expectation.

Your honour's in all duty,
WILLIAM SHAKESPEARE

3

VENUS AND ADONIS

EVEN as the sun with purple-colour'd face
Had ta'en his last leave of the weeping morn,
Rose-cheek'd Adonis hied him to the chase;
Hunting he lov'd, but love he laugh'd to scorn:
    Sick-thoughted Venus makes amain unto him,
    And like a bold-fac'd suitor 'gins to woo him.

"Thrice fairer than myself," thus she began,
"The field's chief flower, sweet above compare,
Stain to all nymphs, more lovely than a man,
More white and red than doves or roses are:
    Nature that made thee, with herself at strife,
    Saith that the world hath ending with thy life.

"Vouchsafe, thou wonder, to alight thy steed,
And rein his proud head to the saddle-bow;
If thou wilt deign this favour, for thy meed
A thousand honey-secrets shalt thou know:
    Here come and sit, where never serpent hisses,
    And being set, I'll smother thee with kisses;

"And yet not cloy thy lips with loath'd satiety,
But rather famish them amid their plenty,
Making them red and pale with fresh variety,—
Ten kisses short as one, one long as twenty:
    A summer's day will seem an hour but short,
    Being wasted in such time-beguiling sport."

With this she seizeth on his sweating palm,
The precedent of pith and livelihood,
And, trembling in her passion, calls it balm,
Earth's sovereign salve to do a goddess good:
    Being so enrag'd, desire doth lend her force
    Courageously to pluck him from his horse.

Over one arm the lusty courser's rein,
Under her other was the tender boy,
Who blush'd and pouted in a dull disdain,
With leaden appetite, unapt to toy;
    She red and hot as coals of glowing fire,
    He red for shame, but frosty in desire.

The studded bridle on a ragged bough
Nimbly she fastens; (O, how quick is love!)
The steed is stalled up, and even now
To tie the rider she begins to prove:
    Backward she push'd him, as she would be thrust,
    And govern'd him in strength, though not in lust.

So soon was she along, as he was down,
Each leaning on their elbows and their hips:
Now doth she stroke his cheek, now doth he frown,
And 'gins to chide, but soon she stops his lips;
    And kissing, speaks, with lustful language broken,
    "If thou wilt chide, thy lips shall never open."

He burns with bashful shame; she with her tears
Doth quench the maiden burning of his cheeks:
Then with her windy sighs and golden hairs,
To fan and blow them dry again she seeks:
    He saith she is immodest, blames her 'miss,
    What follows more she murders with a kiss.

Even as an empty eagle, sharp by fast,
Tires with her beak on feathers, flesh, and bone,
Shaking her wings, devouring all in haste,
Till either gorge be stuff'd, or prey be gone;
    Even so she kiss'd his brow, his cheek, his chin,
    And where she ends she doth anew begin.

Forc'd to content, but never to obey,
Panting he lies, and breatheth in her face;
She feedeth on the steam as on a prey,
And calls it heavenly moisture, air of grace;
    Wishing her cheeks were gardens full of flowers,
    So they were dew'd with such-distilling showers.

Look, how a bird lies tangled in a net,
So fasten'd in her arms Adonis lies;
Pure shame and aw'd resistance made him fret,
Which bred more beauty in his angry eyes:
    Rain added to a river that is rank,
    Perforce will force it overflow the bank.

Still she entreats, and prettily entreats,
For to a pretty ear she tunes her tale;
Still is he sullen, still he low'rs and frets,
'Twixt crimson shame and anger ashy-pale;
    Being red, she loves him best; and being white,
    Her best is better'd with a more delight.

Look how he can, she cannot choose but love;
And by her fair immortal hand she swears
From his soft bosom never to remove,
Till he take truce with her contending tears,
    Which long have rain'd, making her cheeks all wet;
    And one sweet kiss shall pay this countless debt.

Upon this promise did he raise his chin,
Like a dive-dapper peering through a wave,
Who, being look'd on, ducks as quickly in;
So offers he to give what she did crave;
    But when her lips were ready for his pay,
    He winks, and turns his lips another way.

Never did passenger in summer's heat
More thirst for drink than she for this good turn:
Her help she sees, but help she cannot get;
She bathes in water, yet her fire must burn:
    "O, pity," 'gan she cry, "flint-hearted boy!
    'Tis but a kiss I beg; why art thou coy?

"I have been woo'd, as I entreat thee now,
Even by the stern and direful god of war,
Whose sinewy neck in battle ne'er did bow,
Who conquers where he comes, in every jar;
    Yet hath he been my captive and my slave,
    And begg'd for that which thou unask'd shalt have.

"Over my altars hath he hung his lance,
His batter'd shield, his uncontrolled crest,
And for my sake hath learn'd to sport and dance,
To toy, to wanton, dally, smile, and jest;
    Scorning his churlish drum, and ensign red,
    Making my arms his field, his tent my bed.

"Thus he that overrul'd I oversway'd,
Leading him prisoner in a red-rose chain:
Strong-temper'd steel his stronger strength obey'd,
Yet was he servile to my coy disdain.
    O, be not proud, nor brag not of thy might,
    For mastering her that foil'd the god of fight!

"Touch but my lips with those fair lips of thine,—
Though mine be not so fair, yet are they red,—
The kiss shall be thine own as well as mine:—
What see'st thou in the ground? hold up thy head;
    Look in mine eyeballs, there thy beauty lies;
    Then why not lips on lips, since eyes in eyes?

"Art thou asham'd to kiss? then wink again,
And I will wink; so shall the day seem night;
Love keeps his revels where there are but twain;
Be bold to play, our sport is not in sight:
    These blue-vein'd violets whereupon we lean
    Never can blab, nor know not what we mean.

"The tender spring upon thy tempting lip
Shows thee unripe: yet mayst thou well be tasted:
Make use of time, let not advantage slip;
Beauty within itself should not be wasted:
    Fair flowers that are not gather'd in their prime
    Rot and consume themselves in little time.

"Were I hard-favour'd, foul, or wrinkled-old,
Ill-natur'd, crooked, churlish, harsh in voice,
O'er-worn, despised, rheumatic, and cold,
Thick-sighted, barren, lean, and lacking juice,
    Then mightst thou pause, for then I were not for thee;
    But having no defects, why dost abhor me?

"Thou canst not see one wrinkle in my brow;
Mine eyes are grey, and bright, and quick in turning;
My beauty as the spring doth yearly grow,
My flesh is soft and plump, my marrow burning;
    My smooth moist hand, were it with thy hand felt,
    Would in thy palm dissolve, or seem to melt.

"Bid me discourse, I will enchant thine ear,
Or, like a fairy, trip upon the green,
Or, like a nymph, with long dishevell'd hair,
Dance on the sands, and yet no footing seen:
    Love is a spirit all compact of fire,
    Not gross to sink, but light, and will aspire.

"Witness this primrose bank whereon I lie;
These forceless flowers like sturdy trees support me;
Two strengthless doves will draw me through the sky,
From morn till night, even where I list to sport me:
    Is love so light, sweet boy, and may it be
    That thou shouldst think it heavy unto thee?

"Is thine own heart to thine own face affected?
Can thy right hand seize love upon thy left?
Then woo thyself, be of thyself rejected,
Steal thine own freedom, and complain on theft.
    Narcissus so himself himself forsook,
    And died to kiss his shadow in the brook.

"Torches are made to light, jewels to wear,
Dainties to taste, fresh beauty for the use,
Herbs for their smell, and sappy plants to bear;
Things growing to themselves are growth's abuse:
  Seeds spring from seeds, and beauty breedeth beauty,
  Thou wast begot,—to get it is thy duty.

"Upon the earth's increase why shouldst thou feed,
Unless the earth with thy increase be fed?
By law of nature thou art bound to breed,
That thine may live, when thou thyself art dead;
  And so, in spite of death, thou dost survive,
  In that thy likeness still is left alive."

By this, the love-sick queen began to sweat,
For, where they lay, the shadow had forsook them,
And Titan, 'tired in the mid-day heat,
With burning eyes did hotly overlook them;
  Wishing Adonis had his team to guide,
  So he were like him, and by Venus' side.

And now Adonis, with a lazy sprite,
And with a heavy, dark, disliking eye,
His lowering brows o'erwhelming his fair sight,
Like misty vapours when they blot the sky,—
  Souring his cheeks, cries, "Fie, no more of love!
  The sun doth burn my face; I must remove."

"Ah me," quoth Venus, "young, and so unkind?
What bare excuses mak'st thou to be gone!
I'll sigh celestial breath, whose gentle wind
Shall cool the heat of this descending sun:
  I'll make a shadow for thee of my hairs;
  If they burn too, I'll quench them with my tears.

"The sun that shines from heaven shines but warm,
And, lo, I lie between that sun and thee!
The heat I have from thence doth little harm,
Thine eye darts forth the fire that burneth me;
 And were I not immortal, life were done,
 Between this heavenly and earthly sun.

"Art thou obdurate, flinty, hard as steel,
Nay, more than flint, for stone at rain relenteth?
Art thou a woman's son, and canst not feel
What 'tis to love? how want of love tormenteth?
 O, had thy mother borne so hard a mind,
 She had not brought forth thee, but died unkind!

"What am I, that thou shouldst contemn me this?
Or what great danger swells upon my suit?
What were thy lips the worse for one poor kiss?
Speak, fair; but speak fair words, or else be mute:
 Give me one kiss, I'll give it thee again,
 And one for interest, if thou wilt have twain.

"Fie, lifeless picture, cold and senseless stone,
Well-painted idol, image dull and dead,
Statue, contenting but the eye alone,
Thing like a man, but of no woman bred!
 Thou art no man, though of a man's complexion,
 For men will kiss even by their own direction."

This said, impatience chokes her pleading tongue,
And swelling passion doth provoke a pause;
Red cheeks and fiery eyes blaze forth her wrong,
Being judge in love, she cannot right her cause:
 And now she weeps, and now she fain would speak,
 And now her sobs do her intendments break.

Sometimes she shakes her head, and then his hand,
Now gazeth she on him, now on the ground;
Sometimes her arms infold him like a band:
She would, he will not in her arms be bound;
 And when from thence he struggles to be gone,
 She locks her lily fingers one in one.

"Fondling," she said, "since I have hemm'd thee here,
Within the circuit of this ivory pale,
I'll be a park, and thou shalt be my deer;
Feed where thou wilt, on mountain or in dale:
 Graze on my lips; and if those hills be dry,
 Stray lower, where the pleasant fountains lie.

"Within this limit is relief enough,
Sweet bottom-grass, and high-delightful plain,
Round rising hillocks, brakes obscure and rough,
To shelter thee from tempest and from rain:
 Then be my deer, since I am such a park;
 No dog shall rouse thee, though a thousand bark."

At this Adonis smiles as in disdain,
That in each cheek appears a pretty dimple:
Love made those hollows, if himself were slain,
He might be buried in a tomb so simple;
 Foreknowing well, if there he came to lie,
 Why, there Love liv'd, and there he could not die.

These lovely caves, these round enchanting pits,
Open'd their mouths to swallow Venus' liking:
Being mad before, how doth she now for wits?
Struck dead at first, what needs a second striking?
 Poor queen of love, in thine own law forlorn,
 To love a cheek that smiles at thee in scorn!

Now which way shall she turn? what shall she say?
Her words are done, her woes the more increasing;
The time is spent, her object will away,
And from her twining arms doth urge releasing:
    "Pity," she cries, "some favour—some remorse!"
    Away he springs, and hasteth to his horse.

But, lo, from forth a copse that neighbours by,
A breeding jennet, lusty, young, and proud,
Adonis' trampling courser doth espy,
And forth she rushes, snorts, and neighs aloud:
    The strong-neck'd steed, being tied unto a tree,
    Breaketh his rein, and to her straight goes he.

Imperiously he leaps, he neighs, he bounds,
And now his woven girths he breaks asunder;
The bearing earth with his hard hoof he wounds,
Whose hollow womb resounds like heaven's thunder:
    The iron bit he crushes 'tween his teeth,
    Controlling what he was controlled with.

His ears up-prick'd; his braided hanging mane
Upon his compass'd crest now stand on end;
His nostrils drink the air, and forth again,
As from a furnace, vapours doth he send:
    His eye, which scornfully glisters like fire,
    Shows his hot courage and his high desire.

Sometime he trots, as if he told the steps,
With gentle majesty and modest pride;
Anon he rears upright, curvets and leaps,
As who should say, Lo, thus my strength is tried,
    And this I do to captivate the eye
    Of the fair breeder that is standing by.

What recketh he his rider's angry stir,
His flattering "Holla," or his "Stand, I say"?
What cares he now for curb or pricking spur?
For rich caparisons or trapping gay?
    He sees his love, and nothing else he sees,
    Nor nothing else with his proud sight agrees.

Look, when a painter would surpass the life,
In limning out a well-proportioned steed,
His art with nature's workmanship at strife,
As if the dead the living should exceed;
    So did this horse excel a common one,
    In shape, in courage, colour, pace, and bone.

Round-hoof'd, short-jointed, fetlocks shag and long,
Broad breast, full eye, small head, and nostril wide,
High crest, short ears, straight legs, and passing strong
Thick mane, thick tail, broad buttock, tender hide:
    Look, what a horse should have he did not lack,
    Save a proud rider on so proud a back.

Sometimes he scuds far off, and there he stares;
Anon he starts at stirring of a feather;
To bid the wind a base he now prepares,
And whêr he run or fly they know not whether;
    For through his mane and tail the high wind sings,
    Fanning the hairs, who wave like feather'd wings.

He looks upon his love, and neighs unto her;
She answers him, as if she knew his mind:
Being proud, as females are, to see him woo her,
She puts on outward strangeness, seems unkind;
    Spurns at his love, and scorns the heat he feels,
    Beating his kind embracements with her heels.

Then, like a melancholy malcontent,
He vails his tail, that, like a falling plume,
Cool shadow to his melting buttock lent:
He stamps, and bites the poor flies in his fume.
  His love, perceiving how he is enrag'd,
  Grew kinder, and his fury was assuag'd.

His testy master goeth about to take him;
When, lo, the unback'd breeder, full of fear,
Jealous of catching, swiftly doth forsake him,
With her horse, and left Adonis there:
  As they were mad, unto the wood they hie them,
  Out-stripping crows that strive to over-fly them.

All swoln with chafing down Adonis sits,
Banning his boisterous and unruly beast:
And now the happy season once more fits,
That love-sick Love by pleading may be blest;
  For lovers say, the heart hath treble wrong
  When it is barr'd the aidance of the tongue.

An oven that is stopp'd, or river stay'd,
Burneth more hotly, swelleth more with rage:
So of concealed sorrow may be said;
Free vent of words love's fire doth assuage;
  But when the heart's attorney once is mute,
  The client breaks, as desperate in his suit.

He sees her coming, and begins to glow,
Even as a dying coal revives with wind,
And with his bonnet hides his angry brow;
Looks on the dull earth with disturbed mind;
  Taking no notice that she is so nigh,
  For all askance he holds her in his eye.

O, what a sight it was, wistly to view
How she came stealing to the wayward boy!
To note the fighting conflict of her hue,
How white and red each other did destroy!
    But now her cheek was pale, and by and by
    It flash'd forth fire, as lightning from the sky.

Now was she just before him as he sat,
And like a lowly lover down she kneels;
With one fair hand she heaveth up his hat,
Her other tender hand his fair cheek feels:
    His tenderer cheek receives her soft hand's print,
    As apt as new-fall'n snow takes any dint.

O, what a war of looks was there between them!
Her eyes, petitioners, to his eyes suing;
His eyes saw her eyes as they had not seen them;
Her eyes woo'd still, his eyes disdain'd the wooing:
    And all this dumb play had his acts made plain
    With tears, which, chorus-like, her eyes did rain.

Full gently now she takes him by the hand,
A lily prison'd in a gaol of snow,
Or ivory in an alabaster band;
So white a friend engirts so white a foe:
    This beauteous combat, wilful and unwilling,
    Show'd like two silver doves that sit a-billing.

Once more the engine of her thoughts began:
"O, fairest mover on this mortal round,
Would thou wert as I am, and I a man,
My heart as whole as thine, thy heart my wound;
    For one sweet look thy help I would assure thee,
    Though nothing but my body's bane would cure thee."

"Give me my hand," said he, "why dost thou feel it?"
"Give me my heart," said she, "and thou shalt have it;
O, give it me, lest thy hard heart do steel it,
And being steel'd, soft sighs can never grave it:
    Then love's deep groans I never shall regard,
    Because Adonis' heart hath made mine hard."

"For shame," he cries, "let go, and let me go;
My day's delight is past, my horse is gone,
and 'tis your fault I am bereft him so;
I pray you hence, and leave me here alone;
    For all my mind, my thought, my busy care,
    Is how to get my palfrey from the mare."

Thus she replies: "Thy palfrey, as he should,
Welcomes the warm approach of sweet desire:
Affection is a coal that must be cool'd;
Else, suffer'd, it will set the heart on fire:
    The sea hath bounds, but deep desire hath none;
    Therefore no marvel though thy horse be gone.

"How like a jade he stood, tied to the tree,
Servilely master'd with a leathern rein!
But when he saw his love, his youth's fair fee,
He held such petty bondage in disdain;
    Throwing the base thong from his bending crest,
    Enfranchising his mouth, his back, his breast.

"Who sees his true-love in her naked bed
Teaching the sheets a whiter hue than white,
But, when his glutton eye so full hath fed,
His other agents aim at like delight?
    Who is so faint that dare not be bold
    To touch the fire, the weather being cold?

"Let me excuse thy courser, gentle boy;
And learn of him, I heartily beseech thee,
To take advantage on presented joy;
Though I were dumb, yet his proceedings teach thee:
    O, learn to love! the lesson is but plain,
    And once made perfect, never lost again."

"I know not love," quoth he, "nor will not know it,
Unless it be a boar, and then I chase it;
'Tis much to borrow, and I will not owe it;
My love to love is love but to disgrace it;
    For I have heard it is a life in death,
    That laughs, that weeps, and all but with a breath.

"Who wears a garment shapeless and unfinish'd?
Who plucks the bud before one leaf put forth?
If springing things be any jot diminish'd,
They wither in their prime, prove nothing worth:
    The colt that's back'd and burden'd being young,
    Loseth his pride, and never waxeth strong.

"You hurt my hand with wringing; let us part,
And leave this idle theme, this bootless chat:
Remove your siege from my unyielding heart;
To love's alarms it will not ope the gate:
    Dismiss your vows, your feigned tears, your flattery;
    For where a heart is hard, they make no battery."

"What! canst thou talk," quoth she, "hast thou a tongue?
O, would thou hadst not, or I had no hearing!
Thy mermaid's voice hath done me double wrong;
I had my load before, now press'd with bearing:
    Melodious discord, heavenly tune harsh-sounding,
    Earth's deep-sweet music, and heart's deep-sore wounding.

"Had I no eyes but ears, my ears would love
That inward beauty and invisible;
Or were I deaf, thy outward parts would move
Each part in me that were but sensible:
    Though neither eyes nor ears, to hear nor see,
    Yet should I be in love by touching thee.

"Say, that the sense of feeling were bereft me,
And that I could not see, nor hear, nor touch,
And nothing but the very smell were left me,
Yet would my love to thee be still as much;
    For from the still'tory of thy face excelling
    Comes breath perfum'd, that breedeth love by smelling.

"But O, what banquet wert thou to the taste,
Being nurse and feeder of the other four!
Would they not wish the feast might ever last,
And bid Suspicion double-lock the door?
    Lest Jealousy, that sour unwelcome guest,
    Should, by his stealing in, disturb the feast."

Once more the ruby-colour'd portal open'd,
Which to his speech did honey passage yield;
Like a red morn, that ever yet betoken'd
Wreck to the seaman, tempest to the field,
    Sorrow to shepherds, woe unto the birds,
    Gusts and foul flaws to herdmen and to herds.

This ill presage advisedly she marketh:
Even as the wind is hush'd before it raineth,
Or as the wolf doth grin before he barketh,
Or as the berry breaks before it staineth,
    Or like the deadly bullet of a gun,
    His meaning struck her ere his words begun.

And at his look she flatly falleth down,
For looks kill love, and love by looks reviveth;
A smile recures the wounding of a frown;
But blessed bankrupt, that by love so thriveth!
    The silly boy, believing she is dead,
      Claps her pale cheek, till clapping makes it red;

And all-amaz'd brake off his late intent,
For sharply did he think to reprehend her,
Which cunning love did wittily prevent:
Fair fall the wit that can so well defend her!
    For on the grass she lies as she were slain,
      Till his breath breatheth life in her again.

He wrings her nose, he strikes her on the cheeks,
He bends her fingers, holds her pulses hard,
He chafes her lips; a thousand ways he seeks
To mend the hurt that his unkindness marr'd:
    He kisses her; and she, by her good will,
      Will never rise, so he will kiss her still.

The night of sorrow now is turn'd to day:
Her two blue windows faintly she up-heaveth,
Like the fair sun, when in his fresh array
He cheers the morn, and all the earth relieveth:
    And as the bright sun glorifies the sky,
      So is her face illumin'd with her eye;

Whose beams upon his hairless face are fix'd,
As if from thence they borrow'd all their shine.
Were never four such lamps together mix'd,
Had not his clouded with his brows' repine;
    But hers, which through the crystal tears gave light,
      Shone like the moon in water seen by night.

"O, where am I?" quoth she, "in earth or heaven,
Or in the ocean drench'd, or in the fire?
What hour is this? or morn or weary even?
Do I delight to die, or life desire?
　　But now I liv'd, and life was death's annoy;
　　But now I died, and death was lively joy.

"O, thou didst kill me, kill me once again:
Thy eyes' shrewd tutor, that hard heart of thine,
Hath taught them scornful tricks, and such disdain,
That they have murder'd this poor heart of mine;
　　And these mine eyes, true leaders to their queen,
　　But for thy piteous lips no more had seen.

"Long may they kiss each other, for this cure!
O, never let their crimson liveries wear!
And as they last, their verdure still endure,
To drive infection from the dangerous year!
　　That the star-gazers, having writ on death,
　　May say, the plague is banish'd by thy breath.

"Pure lips, sweet seals in my soft lips imprinted,
What bargains may I make, still to be sealing?
To sell myself I can be well contented,
So thou wilt buy, and pay, and use good dealing;
　　Which purchase if thou make, for fear of slips
　　Set thy seal-manual on my wax-red lips.

"A thousand kisses buys my heart from me;
And pays them at thy leisure, one by one.
What is ten hundred kisses unto thee?
Are they not quickly told, and quickly gone?
　　Say, for non-payment that the debt should double,
　　Is twenty hundred kisses such a trouble?"

"Fair queen," quoth he, "if any love you owe me,
Measure my strangeness with my unripe years;
Before I know myself, seek not to know me;
No fisher but the ungrown fry forbears:
    The mellow plum doth fall, the green sticks fast,
    Or being early pluck'd is sour to taste.

"Look, the world's comforter, with weary gait,
His day's hot task hath ended in the west:
The owl, night's herald, shrieks,—'tis very late;
The sheep are gone to fold, birds to their nest;
    And coal-black clouds that shadow heaven's light
    Do summon us to part, and bid good night.

"Now let me say 'Good night,' and so say you;
If you will say so, you shall have a kiss."
"Good night" quoth she; and, ere he says "Adieu,"
The honey fee of parting tender'd is:
    Her arms do lend his neck a sweet embrace
    Incorporate then they seem; face grows to face;

Till, breathless, he disjoin'd, and backward drew
The heavenly moisture, that sweet coral mouth,
Whose precious taste her thirsty lips well knew,
Whereon they surfeit, yet complain on drought:
    He with her plenty press'd, she faint with dearth,
    (Their lips together glu'd,) fall to the earth.

Now quick Desire hath caught the yielding prey,
And glutton-like she feeds, yet never filleth;
Her lips are conquerors, his lips obey,
Paying what ransom the insulter willeth;
    Whose vulture thought doth pitch the price so high,
    That she will draw his lips' rich treasure dry.

And having felt the sweetness of the spoil,
With blindfold fury she begins to forage;
Her face doth reek and smoke, her blood doth boil,
And careless lust stirs up a desperate courage;
    Planting oblivion, beating reason back,
    Forgetting shame's pure blush and honour's wrack.

Hot, faint, and weary, with her hard embracing,
Like a wild bird being tam'd with too much handling,
Or as the fleet-foot roe that's tir'd with chasing,
Or like the froward infant still'd with dandling,
    He now obeys, and now no more resisteth,
    While she takes all she can, not all she listeth.

What wax so frozen but dissolves with tempering,
And yields at last to every light impression?
Things out of hope are compass'd oft with venturing,
Chiefly in love, whose leave exceeds commission:
    Affection faints not like a pale-fac'd coward,
    But then woos best when most his choice is froward.

When he did frown, O, had she then gave over,
Such nectar from his lips she had not suck'd.
Foul words and frowns must not repel a lover;
What though the rose have prickles, yet 'tis plucked:
    Were beauty under twenty locks kept fast,
    Yet love breaks through, and picks them all at last.

For pity now she can no more detain him;
The poor fool prays her that he may depart:
She is resolv'd no longer to restrain him;
Bids him farewell, and look well to her heart,
    The which, by Cupid's bow she doth protest,
    He carries thence incaged in his breast.

"Sweet boy," she says, "this night I'll waste in sorrow,
For my sick heart commands mine eyes to watch.
Tell me, Love's master, shall we meet to-morrow?
Say, shall we? shall we? wilt thou make the match?"
    He tells her, no; to-morrow he intends
    To hunt the boar with certain of his friends.

"The boar!" quoth she; whereat a sudden pale,
Like lawn being spread upon the blushing rose,
Usurps her cheek; she trembles at his tale,
And on his neck her yoking arms she throws:
    She sinketh down, still hanging by his neck,
    He on her belly falls, she on her back.

Now she is in the very lists of love,
Her champion mounted for the hot encounter:
All is imaginary she doth prove,
He will not manage her, although he mount her;
    That worse than Tantalus' is her annoy,
    To clip Elysium, and to lack her joy.

Even as poor birds, deceiv'd with painted grapes,
Do surfeit by the eye and pine the maw,
Even so she languisheth in her mishaps,
As those poor birds that helpless berries saw.
    The warm effects which she in him finds missing,
    She seeks to kindle with continual kissing.

But all in vain; good queen, it will not be:
She hath assay'd as much as may be prov'd;
Her pleading hath deserv'd a greater fee;
She's Love, she loves, and yet she is not lov'd.
    "Fie, fie," he says, "you crush me; let me go;
    You have no reason to withhold me so."

"Thou hadst been gone," quoth she, "sweet boy, ere this,
But that thou told'st me thou wouldst hunt the boar.
O, be advis'd! thou know'st not what it is
With javelin's point a churlish swine to gore,
     Whose tushes never-sheath'd he whetteth still,
     Like to a mortal butcher, bent to kill.

"On his bow-back he hath a battle set
Of bristly pikes, that ever threat his foes;
His eyes like glow-worms shine when he doth fret:
His snout digs sepulchres where'er he goes;
     Being mov'd, he strikes whate'er is in his way,
     And whom he strikes his cruel tushes slay.

"His brawny sides, with hairy bristles arm'd,
Are better proof than thy spear's point can enter;
His short thick neck cannot be easily harm'd;
Being ireful on the lion he will venture:
     The thorny brambles and embracing bushes,
     As fearful of him, part; through whom he rushes.

"Alas, he nought esteems that face of thine,
To which Love's eyes pay tributary gazes;
Nor thy soft hands, sweet lips, and crystal eyne,
Whose full perfection all the world amazes;
     But having thee at vantage,—wondrous dread!—
     Would root these beauties as he roots the mead.

"Oh, let him keep his loathsome cabin still!
Beauty hath nought to do with such foul fiends:
Come not within his danger by this will;
They that thrive well take counsel of their friends.
     When thou didst name the boar, not to dissemble,
     I fear'd thy fortune, and my joints did tremble.

"Didst thou not mark my face? was it not white?
Saw'st thou not signs of fear lurk in mine eye?
Grew I not faint? and fell I not downright?
Within my bosom, whereon thou dost lie,
 My boding heart pants, beats, and takes no rest,
 But, like an earthquake, shakes thee on my breast.

"For where Love reigns, disturbing Jealousy
Doth call himself Affection's sentinel;
Gives false alarms, suggesteth mutiny,
And in a peaceful hour doth cry, 'Kill, kill';
 Distempering gentle Love in his desire,
 As air and water do abate the fire.

"This sour informer, this bate-breeding spy,
This canker that eats up Love's tender spring,
This carry-tale, dissentious Jealousy,
That sometime true news, sometime false doth bring,
 Knocks at my heart, and whispers in mine ear,
 That if I love thee, I thy death should fear:

"And more than so, presenteth to mine eye
The picture of an angry-chafing boar,
Under whose sharp fangs on his back doth lie
An image like thyself, all stain'd with gore;
 Whose blood upon the fresh flowers being shed
 Doth make them droop with grief and hang the head.

"What should I do, seeing thee so indeed,
That tremble at the imagination?
The thought of it doth make my faint heart bleed,
And fear doth teach it divination:
 I prophesy thy death, my living sorrow,
 If thou encounter with the boar to-morrow.

"But if thou needs will hunt, be rul'd by me;
Uncouple at the timorous flying hare,
Or at the fox, which lives by subtlety,
Or at the roe, which no encounter dare:
  Pursue these fearful creatures o'er the downs,
  And on thy well-breath'd horse keep with thy hounds.

"And when thou hast on foot the purblind hare,
Mark the poor wretch, to overshoot his troubles,
How he outruns the wind, and with what care
He cranks and crosses with a thousand doubles:
  The many musits through the which he goes
  Are like a labyrinth to amaze his foes.

"Sometimes he runs among a flock of sheep,
To make the cunning hounds mistake their smell,
And sometimes where earth-delving conies keep,
To stop the loud pursuers in their yell;
  And sometimes sorteth with a herd of deer:
  Danger deviseth shifts; wit waits on fear:

"For there his smell with others being mingled,
The hot scent-snuffing hounds are driven to doubt,
Ceasing their clamorous cry till they have singled
With much ado the cold fault cleanly out;
  Then do they spend their mouths: Echo replies,
  As if another chase were in the skies.

"By this, poor Wat, far off upon a hill,
Stands on his hinder legs with listening ear,
To hearken if his foes pursue him still:
Anon their loud alarums he doth hear;
  And now his grief may be compared well
  To one sore sick that hears the passing-bell.

"Then shalt thou see the dew-bedabbled wretch
Turn, and return, indenting with the way;
Each envious briar his weary legs doth scratch,
Each shadow makes him stop, each murmur stay:
    For misery is trodden on by many,
    And being low never reliev'd by any.

"Lie quietly, and hear a little more;
Nay, do not struggle, for thou shalt not rise:
To make thee hate the hunting of the boar,
Unlike myself thou hear'st me moralize,
    Applying this to that, and so to so;
    For love can comment upon every woe.

"Where did I leave?"—"No matter where," quoth he;
"Leave me, and then the story aptly ends:
The night is spent."—"Why, what of that?" quoth she.
"I am," quoth he, "expected of my friends;
    And now 'tis dark, and going I shall fall."
    "In night," quoth she, "desire sees best of all.

"But if thou fall, O, then imagine this,
The earth in love with thee thy footing trips,
And all is but to rob thee of a kiss.
Rich preys make true-men thieves; so do thy lips
    Make modest Dian cloudy and forlorn,
    Lest she should steal a kiss, and die forsworn.

Now of this dark night I perceive the reason:
Cynthia for shame obscures her silver shine,
Till forging Nature be condemn'd of treason,
For stealing moulds from heaven that were divine,
    Wherein she fram'd thee in high heaven's despite,
    To shame the sun by day, and her by night.

"And therefore hath she brib'd the Destinies,
To cross the curious workmanship of nature,
To mingle beauty with infirmities,
And pure perfection with impure defeature;
    Making it subject to the tyranny
    Of mad mischances and much misery;

"As burning fevers, agues pale and faint,
Life-poisoning pestilence, and frenzies wood,
The marrow-eating sickness, whose attaint
Disorder breeds by heating of the blood:
    Surfeits, imposthumes, grief, and damn'd despair,
    Swear Nature's death for framing thee so fair.

"And not the least of all these maladies,
But in one minute's fight brings beauty under:
Both favour, savour, hue, and qualities,
Whereat the impartial gazer late did wonder,
    Are on the sudden wasted, thaw'd, and done,
    As mountain-snow melts with the mid-day sun.

"Therefore, despite of fruitless chastity,
Love-lacking vestals, and self-loving nuns,
That on the earth would breed a scarcity
And barren dearth of daughters and of sons.
    Be prodigal: the lamp that burns by night
    Dries up his oil to lend the world his light.

"What is thy body but a swallowing grave,
Seeming to bury that posterity
Which by the rights of time thou needs must have,
If thou destroy them not in dark obscurity?
    If so, the world will hold thee in disdain,
    Sith in thy pride so fair a hope is slain.

"So in thyself thyself art made away;
A mischief worse than civil home bred strife,
Or theirs whose desperate hands themselves do slay.
Or butcher-sire, that reaves his son of life.
  Foul-cankering rust the hidden treasure frets,
  But gold that's put to use more gold begets."

"Nay, then," quoth Adon, "you will fall again
Into your idle over-handled theme:
The kiss I gave you is bestowed in vain,
And all in vain you strive against the stream;
  For by this black-fac'd night, desire's foul nurse,
  Your treatise makes me like you worse and worse.

"If love have lent you twenty thousand tongues,
And every tongue more moving than your own,
Bewitching like the wanton mermaid's songs,
Yet from mine ear the tempting tune is blown;
  For know, my heart stands armed in mine ear,
  And will not let a false sound enter there;

"Lest the deceiving harmony should run
Into the quiet closure of my breast;
And then my little heart were quite undone,
In his bedchamber be barr'd of rest.
  No, lady, no; my heart longs not to groan,
  But soundly sleeps, while now it sleeps alone.

"What have you urg'd that I cannot reprove?
The path is smooth that leadeth on to danger;
I hate not love, but your device in love,
That lends embracements unto every stranger.
  You do it for increase; O, strange excuse,
  When reason is the bawd to lust's abuse!

"Call it not love, for Love to heaven is fled,
Since sweating Lust on earth usurp'd his name;
Under whose simple semblance he hath fed
Upon fresh beauty, blotting it with blame;
    Which the hot tyrant stains and soon bereaves,
    As caterpillars do the tender leaves.

"Love comforteth like sunshine after rain,
But Lust's effect is tempest after sun;
Love's gentle spring doth always fresh remain,
Lust's winter comes ere summer half be done.
    Love surfeits not; Lust like a glutton dies:
    Love is all truth; Lust full of forged lies.

"More I could tell, but more I dare not say;
The text is old, the orator too green:
Therefore, in sadness, now I will away;
My face is full of shame, my heart of teen;
    Mine ears that to your wanton talk attended
    Do burn themselves for having so offended."

With this, he breaketh from the sweet embrace
Of those fair arms which bound him to her breast,
And homeward through the dark laund runs apace;
Leaves Love upon her back deeply distress'd.
    Look, how a bright star shooteth from the sky,
    So glides he in the night from Venus' eye;

Which after him she darts, as one on shore
Gazing upon a late-embarked friend,
Till the wild waves will have him seen no more,
Whose ridges with the meeting clouds contend;
    So did the merciless and pitchy night
    Fold in the object that did feed her sight.

Whereat amaz'd, as one that unaware
Hath dropp'd a precious jewel in the flood,
Or 'stonish'd as night-wanderers often are,
Their light blown out in some mistrustful wood;
    Even so confounded in the dark she lay,
    Having lost the fair discovery of her way.

And now she beats her heart, whereat it groans,
That all the neighbour-caves, as seeming troubled,
Make verbal repetition of her moans;
Passion on passion deeply is redoubled:
    "Ah me!" she cries, and twenty times, "Woe, woe!"
    And twenty echoes twenty times cry so.

She, marking them, begins a wailing note,
And sings extemp'rally a woeful ditty;
How love makes young men thrall, and old men dote;
How love is wise in folly, foolish-witty:
    Her heavy anthem still concludes in "Woe,"
    And still the choir of echoes answer so.

Her song was tedious, and outwore the night,
For lovers' hours are long, though seeming short:
If pleas'd themselves, others, they think, delight
In such-like circumstances, with such-like sport:
    Their copious stories, oftentimes begun,
    End without audience, and are never done.

For who hath she to spend the night withal,
But idle, sounds-resembling, parasites;
Like shrill-tongued tapsters answering every call,
Soothing the humour of fantastic wits?
    She says, "'Tis so:" they answer all, "'Tis so;"
    And would say after her, if she said "No." .

Lo, here the gentle lark, weary of rest,
From his moist cabinet mounts up on high,
And wakes the morning, from whose silver breast
The sun ariseth in his majesty;
    Who doth the world so gloriously behold,
    That cedar-tops and hills seem burnish'd gold.

Venus salutes him with this fair Good-morrow:—
"O, thou clear god, and patron of all light,
From whom each lamp and shining star doth borrow
The beauteous influence that makes him bright,
    There lives a son, that suck'd an earthly mother,
    May lend thee light, as thou dost lend to other."

This said, she hasteth to a myrtle grove,
Musing the morning is so much o'erworn,
And yet she hears no tidings of her love:
She hearkens for his hounds and for his horn:
    Anon she hears them chant it lustily,
    And all in haste she coasteth to the cry.

And as she runs, the bushes in the way
Some catch her by the neck, some kiss her face,
Some twin'd about her thigh to make her stay;
She wildly breaketh from their strict embrace,
    Like a milch doe, whose swelling dugs do ache,
    Hasting to feed her fawn hid in some brake.

By this, she hears the hounds are at a bay;
Whereat she starts, like one that spies an adder
Wreath'd up in fatal folds just in his way,
The fear whereof doth make him shake and shudder;
    Even so the timorous yelping of the hounds
    Appals her senses, and her spirit confounds.

For now she knows it is no gentle chase,
But the blunt boar, rough bear, or lion proud,
Because the cry remaineth in one place,
Where fearfully the dogs exclaim aloud:
    Finding their enemy to be so curst,
    They all strain court'sy who shall cope him first.

This dismal cry rings sadly in her ear,
Through which it enters to surprise her heart;
Who, overcome by doubt and bloodless fear,
With cold-pale weakness numbs each feeling part:
    Like soldiers when their captain once doth yield,
    They basely fly, and dare not stay the field.

Thus stands she in a trembling ecstasy;
Till, cheering up her senses all-dismay'd,
She tells them 't is a causeless fantasy,
And childish error, that they are afraid;
    Bids them leave quaking, bids them fear no more:—
    And with that word she spied the hunted boar;

Whose frothy mouth, bepainted all with red,
Like milk and blood being mingled both together,
A second fear through all her sinews spread,
Which madly hurries her she knows not whither:
    This way she runs, and now she will no further,
    But back retires to rate the boar for murther.

A thousand spleens bear her a thousand ways;
She treads the path that she untreads again;
Her more than haste is mated with delays,
Like the proceedings of a drunken brain,
    Full of respects yet nought at all respecting,
    In hand with all things, nought at all effecting.

Here kennell'd in a brake she finds a hound,
. And asks the weary caitiff for his master;
And there another licking of his wound,
'Gainst venom'd sores the only sovereign plaster;
    And here she meets another sadly scowling,
    To whom she speaks, and he replies with howling.

When he hath ceas'd his ill-resounding noise,
Another flap-mouth'd mourner, black and grim,
Against the welkin volleys out his voice;
Another and another answer him,
    Clapping their proud tails to the ground below,
    Shaking their scratch'd ears, bleeding as they go.

Look, how the world's poor people are amaz'd
At apparitions, signs, and prodigies,
Whereon with fearful eyes they long have gaz'd,
Infusing them with dreadful prophecies;
    So she at these sad signs draws up her breath,
    And, sighing it again, exclaims on Death:

"Hard-favour'd tyrant, ugly, meagre, lean,
Hateful divorce of love,"—thus chides she Death—
"Grim-grinning ghost, earth's worm, what dost thou mean
To stifle beauty and to steal his breath,
    Who when he liv'd, his breath and beauty set
    Gloss on the rose, smell to the violet?

"If he be dead,—O, not, it cannot be,
Seeing his beauty, thou shouldst strike at it!—
O yes, it may! thou hast no eyes to see,
But hatefully at random dost thou hit:
    Thy mark is feeble age; but thy false dart
    Mistakes that aim, and cleaves an infant's heart.

"Hadst thou but bid beware, then he had spoke,
And hearing him, thy power had lost his power.
The Destinies will curse thee for this stroke;
They bid thee crop a weed, thou pluck'st a flower:
  Love's golden arrow at him should have fled,
  And not Death's ebon dart, to strike him dead.

"Dost thou drink tears, that thou provok'st such weeping?
What may a heavy groan advantage thee?
Why hast thou cast into eternal sleeping
Those eyes that taught all other eyes to see?
  Now Nature cares not for thy mortal vigour,
  Since her best work is ruin'd with thy rigour."

Here overcome, as one full of despair,
She vail'd her eyelids, who, like sluices, stopp'd
The crystal tide that from her two cheeks fair
In the sweet channel of her bosom dropp'd;
  But through the flood-gates break the silver rain,
  And with his strong course opens them again.

O, how her eyes and tears did lend and borrow!
Her eyes seen in the tears, tears in her eye;
Both crystals, where they view'd each other's sorrow,—
Sorrow that friendly sighs sought still to dry;
  But like a stormy day, now wind, now rain,
  Sighs dry her cheeks, tears make them wet again.

Variable passions throng her constant woe,
As striving who should best become her grief;
All entertain'd, each passion labours so,
That every present sorrow seemeth chief,
  But none is best; then join they all together,
  Like many clouds consulting for foul weather.

By this, far off she hears some huntsman hollo;
A nurse's song ne'er pleas'd her babe so well:
The dire imagination she did follow
This sound of hope doth labour to expel;
    For now reviving joy bids her rejoice,
    And flatters her it is Adonis' voice.

Whereat her tears began to turn their tide,
Being prison'd in her eye, like pearls in glass;
Yet sometimes fall an orient drop beside,
Which her cheek melts, as scorning it should pass,
    To wash the foul face of the sluttish ground,
    Who is but drunken when she seemeth drown'd.

O, hard-believing love, how strange it seems
Not to believe, and yet too credulous!
Thy weal and woe are both of them extremes;
Despair and hope make thee ridiculous:
    The one doth flatter thee in thoughts unlikely,
    In likely thoughts the other kills thee quickly.

Now she unweaves the web that she hath wrought;
Adonis lives, and Death is not to blame;
It was not she that call'd him all to-naught;
Now she adds honours to his hateful name;
    She clepes him king of graves, and grave for kings,
    Imperious supreme of all mortal things.

"No, no," quoth she, "sweet Death, I did but jest;
Yet pardon me, I felt a kind of fear
Whenas I met the boar, that bloody beast,
Which knows no pity, but is still severe;
    Then, gentle shadow,—truth I must confess,—
    I rail'd on thee, fearing my love's decease.

"'Tis not my fault: the boar provok'd my tongue;
Be wreak'd on him, invisible commander;
'Tis he, foul creature, that hath done thee wrong;
I did but act, he's author of thy slander.
     Grief hath two tongues, and never woman yet,
     Could rule them both, without ten women's wit."

Thus, hoping that Adonis is alive,
Her rash suspect she doth extenuate;
And that his beauty may the better thrive,
With Death she humbly doth insinuate;
     Tells him of trophies, statues, tombs, and stories
     His victories, his triumphs, and his glories.

"O, Jove," quoth she, "how much a fool was I,
To be of such a weak and silly mind,
To wail his death who lives, and must not die
Till mutual overthrow of mortal kind!
     For he being dead, with him is beauty slain,
     And, beauty dead, black chaos comes again.

"Fie, fie, fond love, thou art so full of fear
As one with treasure laden, hemm'd with thieves;
Trifles, unwitnessed with eye or ear,
Thy coward heart with false bethinking grieves."
     Even at this word she hears a merry horn,
     Whereat she leaps that was but late forlorn.

As falcon to the lure, away she flies;
The grass stoops not, she treads on it so light;
And in her haste unfortunately spies
The foul boar's conquest on her fair delight;
     Which seen, her eyes, as murder'd with the view,
     Like stars asham'd of day, themselves withdrew;

Or, as the snail, whose tender horns being hit,
Shrinks backward in his shelly cave with pain,
And there, all smother'd up, in shade doth sit,
Long after fearing to creep forth again;
  So, at his bloody view, her eyes are fled
  Into the deep-dark cabins of her head;

Where they resign their office and their light
To the disposing of her troubled brain;
Who bids them still consort with ugly night,
And never wound the heart with looks again;
  Who, like a king perplexed in his throne,
  By their suggestion gives a deadly groan,

Whereat each tributary subject quakes;
As when the wind, imprison'd in the ground,
Struggling for passage, earth's foundation shakes,
Which with cold terror doth men's minds confound,
  This mutiny each part doth so surprise,
  That from their dark beds once more leap her eyes;

And, being open'd, threw unwilling light
Upon the wide wound that the boar had trench'd
In his soft flank; whose wonted lily white
With purple tears, that his wound wept, was drench'd:
  No flower was nigh, no grass, herb, leaf, or weed,
  But stole his blood, and seem'd with him to bleed.

This solemn sympathy poor Venus noteth;
Over one shoulder doth she hang her head;
Dumbly she passions, franticly she doteth;
She thinks he could not die, he is not dead:
  Her voice is stopp'd, her joints forget to bow;
  Her eyes are mad that they have wept till now.

Upon his hurt she looks so steadfastly
That her sight dazzling makes the wound seem three;
And then she reprehends her mangling eye
That makes more gashes where no breach should be:
    His face seems twain, each several limb is doubled;
    For oft the eye mistakes, the brain being troubled.

"My tongue cannot express my grief for one,
And yet," quoth she, "behold two Adons dead!
My sighs are blown away, my salt tears gone,
Mine eyes are turn'd to fire, my heart to lead:
    Heavy heart's lead melt at mine eyes' red fire!
    So shall I die by drops of hot desire.

"Alas, poor world, what treasure has thou lost!
What face remains alive that's worth the viewing?
Whose tongue is music now? what canst thou boast
Of things long since, or any thing ensuing?
    The flowers are sweet, their colours fresh and trim;
    But true-sweet beauty liv'd and died with him.

"Bonnet nor veil henceforth no creature wear!
Nor sun nor wind will ever strive to kiss you:
Having no fair to lose, you need not fear;
The sun doth scorn you, and the wind doth hiss you:
    But when Adonis liv'd, sun and sharp air
    Lurk'd like two thieves to rob him of his fair;

"And therefore would he put his bonnet on,
Under whose brim the gaudy sun would peep;
The wind would blow it off, and, being gone,
Play with his locks; then would Adonis weep;
    And straight, in pity of his tender years,
    They both would strive who first should dry his tears.

"To see his face the lion walk'd along
Behind some hedge, because he would not fear him;
To recreate himself, when he hath sung,
The tiger would be tame, and gently hear him;
 If he had spoke, the wolf would leave his prey,
 And never fright the silly lamb that day.

"When he beheld his shadow in the brook,
The fishes spread on it their golden gills;
When he was by, the birds such pleasure took,
That some would sing, some other in their bills
 Would bring him mulberries and ripe-red cherries.
 He fed them with his sight, they him with berries.

"But this foul, grim, and urchin-snouted boar,
Whose downward eye still looketh for a grave,
Ne'er saw the beauteous livery that he wore;
Witness the entertainment that he gave;
 If he did see his face, why then I know
 He thought to kiss him, and hath kill'd him so.

"'Tis true, 'tis true; thus was Adonis slain:
He ran upon the boar with his sharp spear,
Who did not whet his teeth at him again,
But by a kiss thought to persuade him there;
 And nuzzling in his flank, the loving swine
 Sheath'd, unaware, the tusk in his soft groin.

"Had I been tooth'd like him, I must confess,
With kissing him I should have kill'd him first;
But he is dead, and never did he bless
My youth with his,—the more am I accurst."
 With this, she falleth in the place she stood,
 And stains her face with his congealed blood.

She looks upon his lips, and they are pale;
She takes him by the hand, and that is cold;
She whispers in his ears a heavy tale,
As if they heard the woeful words she told;
    She lifts the coffer-lids that close his eyes,
    Where, lo, two lamps, burnt out, in darkness lies!

Two glasses, where herself herself beheld
A thousand times, and now no more reflect;
Their virtue lost, wherein they late excell'd,
And every beauty robb'd of his effect:
    "Wonder of time," quoth she, "this is my spite,
    That, thou being dead, the day should yet be light.

"Since thou art dead, lo, here I prophesy,
Sorrow on love hereafter shall attend!
It shall be waited on with jealousy,
Find sweet beginning, but unsavoury end;
    Ne'er settled equally, but high or low;
    That all love's pleasure shall not match his woe.

"It shall be fickle, false, and full of fraud;
Bud and be blasted in a breathing-while;
The bottom poison, and the top o'erstraw'd
With sweets that shall the truest sight beguile:
    The strongest body shall it make most weak,
    Strike the wise dumb, and teach the fool to speak.

"It shall be sparing, and too full of riot;
Teaching decrepit age to tread the measures,
The staring ruffian shall it keep in quiet;
Pluck down the rich, enrich the poor with treasures;
    It shall be raging-mad, and silly-mild,
    Make the young old, the old become a child.

"It shall suspect where there is no cause of fear;
It shall not fear where it should most mistrust;
It shall be merciful, and too severe,
And most deceiving when it seems most just;
 Perverse it shall be where it shows most toward,
 Put fear to valour, courage to the coward.

"It shall be cause of war and dire events,
And set dissention 'twixt the son and sire;
Subject and servile to all discontents,
As dry combustious matter is to fire;
 Sith in his prime death doth my love destroy,
 They that love best their loves shall not enjoy."

By this, the boy that by her side lay kill'd
Was melted like a vapour from her sight,
And in his blood, that on the ground lay spill'd,
A purple flower sprung up, chequer'd with white,
 Resembling well his pale cheeks, and the blood
 Which in round drops upon their whiteness stood.

She bows her head, the new-sprung flower to smell,
Comparing it to her Adonis' breath;
And says, within her bosom it shall dwell,
Since he himself is reft from her by death:
 She crops the stalk, and in the breach appears
 Green dropping sap, which she compares to tears.

"Poor flower," quoth she, "this was thy father's guise,—
Sweet issue of a more sweet-smelling sire,—
For every little grief to wet his eyes:
To grow unto himself was his desire,
 And so 'tis thine; but know, it is as good
 To wither in my breast as in his blood.

"Here was thy father's bed, here in my breast;
Thou art the next of blood, and 'tis thy right:
Lo, in this hollow cradle take thy rest,
My throbbing heart shall rock thee day and night!
    Where shall not be one minute in an hour
    Wherein I will not kiss my sweet love's flower."

Thus weary of the world, away she hies,
And yokes her silver doves; by whose swift aid
Their mistress, mounted, through the empty skies
In her light chariot quickly is convey'd;
    Holding their course to Paphos, where their queen
    Means to immure herself and not be seen.

FINIS

Lucrece

TO THE

RIGHT HONOURABLE
HENRY WRIOTHESLY,

EARL OF SOUTHAMPTON,
AND BARON OF TICHFIELD

The love I dedicate to your Lordship is without end; whereof this pamphlet, without beginning, is but a superfluous moiety. The warrant I have of your honourable disposition, not the worth of my untutored lines, makes it assured of acceptance. What I have done is yours; what I have to do is yours; being part in all I have devoted yours. Were my worth greater, my duty would show greater; meantime, as it is, it is bound to your Lordship, to whom I wish long life, still lengthened with all happiness.

Your Lordship's in all duty,
WILLIAM SHAKESPEARE

THE ARGUMENT

LUCIUS TARQUINIUS,—for his excessive pride surnamed Superbus,—after he had caused his own father-in-law, Servius Tullius, to be cruelly murdered, and, contrary to the Roman laws and customs, not requiring or staying for the people's suffrages, had possessed himself of the kingdom, went, accompanied with his sons and other noblemen of Rome, to besiege Ardea. During which siege the principal men of the army meeting one evening at the tent of Sextus Tarquinius, the king's son, in their discourses after supper, every one commended the virtues of his own wife; among whom, Collatinus extolled the incomparable chastity of his wife Lucretia. In that pleasant humour they all posted to Rome; and intending, by their secret and sudden arrival, to make trial of that which every one had before avouched, only Collatinus finds his wife (though it were late in the night) spinning amongst her maids: the other ladies were all found dancing and revelling, or in several disports. Whereupon the noblemen yielded Collatinus the victory, and his wife the fame. At that time Sextus Tarquinius, being inflamed with Lucrece' beauty, yet smothering his passions for the present, departed with the rest back to the camp; from whence he shortly after privily withdrew himself, and was (according to his estate) royally entertained and lodged by Lucrece at Collatium. The same night he treacherously stealeth into her chamber, violently ravished her, and in the early morning speedeth away. Lucrece, in this lamentable plight, hastily dispatcheth messengers, one to Rome for her father, another to the camp for Collatine. They came, the one accompanied with Junius Brutus, the other with Publius Valerius; and finding Lucrece attired in mourning habit, demanded the cause of her sorrow. She, first taking an oath of them for her revenge, revealed the actor, and whole manner of his dealing, and withal suddenly stabbed herself. Which done, with one consent they all vowed to root out the whole hated family of the Tarquins; and bearing the dead body to Rome, Brutus acquainted the people with the doer and manner of the vile deed, with a bitter invective against the tyranny of the king; wherewith the people were so moved, that with one consent and a general acclamation, the Tarquins were all exiled, and the state government changed from kings to consuls.

LUCRECE

FROM the besieged Ardea all in post,
Borne by the trustless wings of false desire,
Lust-breathed Tarquin leaves the Roman host,
And to Collatium bears the lightless fire
Which, in pale embers hid, lurks to aspire,
    And girdle with embracing flames the waist
    Of Collatine's fair love, Lucrece the chaste.

Haply that name of "chaste" unhapp'ly set
This bateless edge on his keen appetite;
When Collatine unwisely did not let
To praise the clear unmatched red and white
Which triumph'd in that sky of his delight,
    Where mortal stars, as bright as heaven's beauties
    With pure aspécts did him peculiar duties.

For the night before, in Tarquin's tent,
Unlock'd the treasure of his happy state;
What priceless wealth the heavens had him lent
In the possession of his beauteous mate;
Reckoning his fortune at such high-proud rate,
 That kings might be espoused to more fame,
 But king nor peer to such a peerless dame.

O, happiness enjoy'd but of a few!
And, if possess'd, as soon decay'd and done
As is the morning's silver-melting dew
Against the golden splendour of the sun!
An expir'd date, cancell'd ere well begun:
 Honour and beauty, in the owner's arms,
 Are weakly fortress'd from a world of harms.

Beauty itself doth of itself persuade
The eyes of men without an orator;
What needeth, then, apologies be made
To set forth that which is so singular?
Or why is Collatine the publisher
 Of that rich jewel he should keep unknown
 From thievish ears, because it is his own?

Perchance his boast of Lucrece' sovereignty
Suggested this proud issue of a king;
For by our ears our hearts oft tainted be:
Perchance that envy of so rich a thing,
Braving compare, disdainfully did sting
 His high-pitch'd thoughts, that meaner men should vaunt
 That golden hap which their superiors want.

But some untimely thought did instigate
His all-too-timeless speed, if none of those:

His honour, his affairs, his friends, his state,
Neglected all, with swift intent he goes
To quench the coal which in his liver glows.
　　O rash-false heat, wrapp'd in repentant cold,
　　Thy hasty spring still blasts, and ne'er grows old!

When at Collatium this false lord arriv'd,
Well was he welcom'd by the Roman dame,
Within whose face beauty and virtue striv'd
Which of them both should underprop her fame:
When virtue bragg'd, beauty would blush for shame;
　　When beauty boasted blushes, in despite
　　Virtue would stain that or with silver white.

But beauty, in that white intituled,
From Venus' doves doth challenge that fair field:
Then virtue claims from beauty beauty's red,
Which virtue gave the golden age to gild
Their silver cheeks, and call'd it then their shield;
　　Teaching them thus to use it in the fight,—
　　When shame assail'd, the red should fence the white.

This heraldry in Lucrece' face was seen,
Argu'd by beauty's red and virtue's white:
Of either's colour was the other queen,
Proving from world's minority their right:
Yet their ambition makes them still to fight;
　　The sovereignty of either being so great,
　　That oft they interchange each other's seat.

This silent war of lilies and of roses
Which Tarquin view'd in her fair face's field,
In their pure ranks his traitor eye encloses;
Where, lest between them both it should be kill'd,
The coward captive vanquished doth yield

To those two armies that would let him go,
Rather than triumph in so false a foe.

Now thinks he that her husband's shallow tongue,—
The niggard prodigal that prais'd her so,—
In that high task hath done her beauty wrong,
Which far exceeds his barren skill to show:
Therefore that praise which Collatine doth owe,
    Enchanted Tarquin answers with surmise,
    In silent wonder of still-gazing eyes.

This earthly saint, adored by this devil,
Little suspecteth the false worshipper;
For unstain'd thoughts do seldom dream on evil;
Birds never lim'd no secret bushes fear:
So guiltless she securely gives good cheer
    And reverend welcome to her princely guest
    Whose inward ill no outward harm express'd:

For that he colour'd with his high estate,
Hiding base sin in plaits of majesty;
That nothing in him seem'd inordinate,
Save sometime too much wonder of his eye,
Which, having all, all could not satisfy;
    But poorly rich, so wanteth in his store,
    That, cloy'd with much, he pineth still for more.

But she, that never cop'd with stranger eyes,
Could pick no meaning from their parling looks,
Nor read the subtle-shining secrecies
Writ in the glassy margents of such books:
She touch'd no unknown baits, nor fear'd no hooks;
    Nor could she moralize his wanton sight
    More than his eyes were open'd to the light.

He stories to her ears her husband's fame,
Won in the fields of fruitful Italy;
And decks with praises Collatine's high name,
Made glorious by his manly chivalry
With bruised arms and wreaths of victory:
 Her joy with heav'd-up hand she doth express,
 And, wordless, so greets heaven for his success.

Far from the purpose of his coming thither,
He makes excuses for his being there.
No cloudy show of stormy blustering weather
Doth yet in his fair welkin once appear;
Till sable Night, mother of Dread and Fear,
 Upon the world dim darkness doth display,
 And in her vaulty prison stows the Day.

For then is Tarquin brought unto his bed,
Intending weariness with heavy sprite;
For, after supper, long he questioned
With modest Lucrece, and wore out the night:
Now leaden slumber with life's strength doth fight;
 And every one to rest themselves betake,
 Save thieves, and cares, and troubled minds, that wake.

As one of which doth Tarquin lie revolving
The sundry dangers of his will's obtaining;
Yet ever to obtain his will resolving,
Though weak-built hopes persuade him to abstaining;
Despair to gain doth traffic oft for gaining;
 And when great treasure is the meed propos'd,
 Though death be adjunct, there's no death suppos'd.

Those that much covet are with gain so fond,
That what they have not, that which they possess,

They scatter and unloose it from their bond,
And so, by hoping more, they have but less;
Or, gaining more, the profit of excess
    Is but to surfeit, and such griefs sustain,
    That they prove bankrupt in this poor-rich gain.

The aim of all is but to nurse the life
With honour, wealth, and ease, in waning age;
And in this aim there is such thwarting strife,
That one for all, or all for one we gage:
As life for honour in fell battles' rage,
    Honour for wealth; and oft that wealth doth cost
    The death of all, and all together lost.

So that in venturing ill we leave to be
The things we are for that which we expect;
And this ambitious-foul infirmity,
In having much, torments us with defect
Of that we have: so then we do neglect
    The thing we have, and, all for want of wit,
    Make something nothing by augmenting it.

Such hazard now must doting Tarquin make,
Pawning his honour to obtain his lust;
And for himself himself he must forsake:
Then where is truth, if there be no self-trust?
When shall he think to find a stranger just,
    When he himself himself confounds, betrays
    To slanderous tongues and wretched hateful days?

Now stole upon the time the dead of night,
When heavy sleep had clos'd up mortal eyes:
No comfortable star did lend his light,
No noise but owls' and wolves' death-boding cries;
Now serves the season that they may surprise

The silly lambs: pure thoughts are dead and still,
While lust and murder wake to stain and kill.

And now this lustful lord leap'd from his bed,
Throwing his mantle rudely o'er his arm;
Is madly toss'd between desire and dread;
Th' one sweetly flatters, th' other feareth harm;
But honest Fear, bewitch'd with lust's foul charm,
  Doth too-too oft betake him to retire,
  Beaten away by brain-sick rude Desire.

His falchion on a flint he softly smiteth,
That from the cold stone sparks of fire do fly,
Whereat a waxen torch forthwith he lighteth,
Which must be lode-star to his lustful eye;
And to the flame thus speaks advisedly,
  "As from this cold flint I enforc'd this fire,
  So Lucrece must I force to my desire."

Here pale with fear he doth premeditate
The dangers of his loathsome enterprise,
And in his inward mind he doth debate
What following sorrow may on this arise;
Then looking scornfully, he doth despise
  His naked armour of still-slaughter'd lust,
  And justly thus controls his thoughts unjust:

"Fair torch, burn out thy light, and lend it not
To darken her whose light excelleth thine!
And die, unhallow'd thoughts, before you blot
With your uncleanness that which is divine!
Offer pure incense to so pure a shrine:
  Let fair humanity abhor the deed
  That spots and stains love's modest snow-white weed.

"O shame to knighthood and to shining arms!
O foul dishonour to my household's grave!
O impious act, including all foul harms!
A martial man to be soft fancy's slave
True valour still a true respect should have;
    Then my digression is so vile, so base,
    That it will live engraven in my face.

"Yea, though I die, the scandal will survive,
And be an eye-sore in my golden coat;
Some loathsome dash the herald will contrive,
To cipher me how fondly I did dote;
That my posterity, sham'd with the note,
    Shall curse my bones, and hold it for no sin
    To wish that I their father had not bin.

"What win I, if I gain the thing I seek?
A dream, a breath, a froth of fleeting joy.
Who buys a minute's mirth to wail a week?
Or sells eternity to get a toy?
For one sweet grape who will the vine destroy?
    Or what fond beggar, but to touch the crown,
    Would with the sceptre straight be strucken down?

"If Collatinus dream of my intent,
Will he not wake, and in a desperate rage
Post hither, this vile purpose to prevent?
This siege that hath engirt his marriage,
This blur to youth, this sorrow to the sage,
    This dying virtue, this surviving shame,
    Whose crime will bear an ever-during blame?

"O, what excuse can my invention make,
When thou shalt charge me with so black a deed?

Will not my tongue be mute, my frail joints shake,
Mine eyes forego their light, my false heart bleed?
The guilt being great, the fear doth still exceed;
    And extreme fear can neither fight nor fly,
    But coward-like with trembling terror die.

"Had Collatinus kill'd my son or sire,
Or lain in ambush to betray my life,
Or were he not my dear friend, this desire
Might have excuse to work upon his wife,
As in revenge or quittal of such strife:
    But as he is my kinsman, my dear friend,
    The shame and fault finds no excuse nor end.

"Shameful it is;—ay, if the fact be known:
Hateful it is;—there is no hate in loving:
I'll beg her love;—but she is not her own:
The worst is but denial and reproving:
My will is strong, past reason's weak removing
    Who fears a sentence or an old man's saw
    Shall by a painted cloth be kept in awe."

Thus, graceless, holds he disputation
'Tween frozen conscience and hot-burning will,
And with good thoughts makes dispensation,
Urging the worser sense for vantage still;
Which in a moment doth confound and kill
    All pure effects, and doth so far proceed,
    That what is vile shows like a virtuous deed.

Quoth he, "She took me kindly by the hand,
And gaz'd for tidings in my eager eyes,
Fearing some hard news from the warlike band
Where her beloved Collatinus lies.
O, how her fear did make her colour rise!

First red as roses that on lawn we lay,
Then white as lawn, the roses took away.

"And how her hand, in my hand being lock'd,
Forc'd it to tremble with her loyal fear!
Which struck her sad, and then it faster rock'd,
Until her husband's welfare she did hear;
Whereat she smiled with so sweet a cheer,
    That had Narcissus seen her as she stood,
    Self-love had never drown'd him in the flood.

"Why hunt I, then, for colour or excuses?
All orators are dumb when beauty pleadeth;
Poor wretches have remorse in poor abuses;
Love thrives not in the heart that shadows dreadeth:
Affection is my captain, and he leadeth;
    And when his gaudy banner is display'd,
    The coward fights, and will not be dismay'd.

"Then, childish fear, avaunt! debating, die!
Respect and reason, wait on wrinkled age!
My heart shall never countermand mine eye:
Sad pause and deep regard beseem the sage;
My part is youth, and beats these from the stage:
    Desire my pilot is, beauty my prize;
    Then who fears sinking where such treasure lies?"

As corn o'ergrown by weeds, so heedful fear
Is almost chok'd by unresisted lust.
Away he steals with open listening ear,
Full of foul hope, and full of fond mistrust;
Both which, as servitors to the unjust,
    So cross him with their opposite persuasion,
    That now he vows a league, and now invasion.

Within his thought her heavenly image sits,
And in the self-same seat sits Collatine:
That eye which looks on her confounds his wits;
That eye which him beholds, as more divine,
Unto a view so false will not incline;
> But with a pure appeal seeks to the heart,
> Which once corrupted takes the worser part;

And therein heartens up his servile powers,
Who, flatter'd by their leader's jocund show,
Stuff up his lust, as minutes fill up hours;
And as their captain, so their pride doth grow,
Paying more slavish tribute than they owe.
> By reprobate desire thus madly led,
> The Roman lord marcheth to Lucrece' bed.

The locks between her chamber and his will,
Each one by him enforc'd, retires his ward;
But, as they open, they all rate his ill,
Which drives the creeping thief to some regard;
The threshold grates the door to have him heard;
> Night-wand'ring weasels shriek to see him there;
> They fright him, yet he still pursues his fear.

As each unwilling portal yields him way,
Through little vents and crannies of the place
The wind wars with his torch to make him stay,
And blows the smoke of it into his face,
Extinguishing his conduct in this case;
> But his hot heart, which fond desire doth scorch,
> Puffs forth another wind that fires the torch;

And being lighted, by the light he spies
Lucretia's glove, wherein her needle sticks:

He takes it from the rushes where it lies,
And griping it, the neeld his finger pricks:
As who should say, This glove to wanton tricks
    Is not inur'd; return again in haste;
    Thou see'st our mistress' ornaments are chaste.

But all these poor forbiddings could not stay him;
He in the worst sense construes their denial:
The doors, the wind, the glove, that did delay him,
He takes for accidental things of trial;
Or as those bars which stop the hourly dial,
    Who with a lingering stay his course doth let,
    Till every minute pays the hour his debt.

"So, so," quoth he, "these lets attend the time,
Like little frosts that sometime threat the spring,
To add a more rejoicing to the prime,
And give the sneaped birds more cause to sing.
Pain pays the income of each precious thing;
    Huge rocks, high winds, strong pirates, shelves and sands,
    The merchant fear, ere rich at home he lands."

Now is he come unto the chamber-door,
That shuts him from the heaven of his thought,
Which with a yielding latch, and with no more,
Hath barr'd him from the blessed thing he sought.
So from himself impiety hath wrought,
    That for his prey to pray he doth begin,
    As if the heavens should countenance his sin.

But in the midst of his unfruitful prayer,
Having solicited th' eternal power,
That his foul thoughts might compass his fair fair,
And they would stand auspicious to the hour,
Even there he starts:—quoth he, "I must deflower:

The powers to whom I pray abhor this fact,
How can they, then, assist me in the act?

"Then Love and Fortune be my gods, my guide!
My will is back'd with resolution:
Thoughts are but dreams till their effects be tried;
The blackest sin is clear'd with absolution;
Against love's fire fear's frost hath dissolution.
  The eye of heaven is out, and misty night
  Covers the shame that follows sweet delight."

This said, his guilty hand pluck'd up the latch,
And with his knee the door he opens wide.
The dove sleeps fast that this night-owl will catch:
Thus treason works ere traitors be espied.
Who sees the lurking serpent steps aside;
  But she, sound sleeping, fearing no such thing,
  Lies at the mercy of his mortal sting.

Into the chamber wickedly he stalks,
And gazeth on her yet-unstained bed.
The curtains being close, about he walks,
Rolling his greedy eye-balls is his head:
By their high treason in his heart misled;
  Which gives the watch-word to his hands full soon,
  To draw the cloud that hides the silver moon.

Look, as the fair and fiery-pointed sun,
Rushing from forth a cloud, bereaves our sight;
Even so, the curtain drawn, his eyes begun
To wink, being blinded with a greater light:
Whether it is that she reflects so bright,
  That dazzleth them, or else some shame supposed;
  But blind they are, and keep themselves enclosed.

O, had they in that darksome prison died!
Then had they seen the period of their ill;
Then Collatine again, by Lucrece' side,
In his clear bed might have reposed still:
But they must ope, this blessed league to kill;
    And holy-thoughted Lucrece to their sight
    Must sell her joy, her life, her world's delight.

Her lily hand her rosy cheek lies under,
Cozening the pillow of a lawful kiss;
Who, therefore angry, seems to part in sunder,
Swelling on either side to want his bliss;
Between whose hills her head entombed is:
    Where, like a virtuous monument, she lies,
    To be admir'd of lewd unhallow'd eyes.

Without the bed her other fair hand was,
On the green coverlet; whose perfect white
Show'd like an April daisy on the grass,
With pearly sweat, resembling dew of night.
Her eyes, like marigolds, had sheath'd their light,
    And canopied in darkness sweetly lay,
    Till they might open to adorn the day.

Her hair, like golden threads, play'd with her breath;
O modest wantons! wanton modesty!
Showing life's triumph in the map of death,
And death's dim look in life's mortality:
Each in her sleep themselves so beautify,
    As if between them twain there were no strife,
    But that life liv'd in death, and death in life.

Her breasts, like ivory globes circled with blue,
A pair of maiden worlds unconquered,

Save of their lord no bearing yoke they knew,
And him by oath they truly honoured.
These worlds in Tarquin new ambition bred;
 Who, like a foul usurper, went about
 From this fair throne to heave the owner out.

What could he see, but mightily he noted?
What did he note, but strongly he desir'd?
What he beheld, on that he firmly doted,
And in his will his wilful eye he tir'd.
With more than admiration he admir'd
 Her azure veins, her alabaster skin,
 Her coral lips, her snow-white dimpled chin.

As the grim lion fawneth o'er his prey,
Sharp hunger by the conquest satisfied,
So o'er this sleeping soul doth Tarquin stay,
His rage of lust by gazing qualified;
Slack'd, not suppress'd; for standing by her side,
 His eye, which late this mutiny restrains,
 Unto a greater uproar tempts his veins:

And they, like straggling slaves for pillage fighting,
Obdurate vassals fell exploits effecting,
In bloody death and ravishment delighting,
Nor children's tears nor mother's groans respecting,
Swell in their pride, the onset still expecting:
 Anon his beating heart, alarum striking,
 Gives the hot charge, and bids them do their liking.

His drumming heart cheers up his burning eye,
His eye commends the leading to his hand;
His hand, as proud of such a dignity,
Smoking with pride, march'd on to make his stand
On her bare breast, the heart of all her land;

Whose ranks of blue veins, as his hand did scale,
Left their round turrets destitute and pale.

They, mustering to the quiet cabinet
Where their dear governess and lady lies,
Do tell her she is dreadfully beset,
And fright with confusion of their cries:
She, much amaz'd, breaks ope her lock'd-up eyes,
  Who, peeping forth this tumult to behold,
  Are by his flaming torch dimm'd and controll'd.

Imagine her as one in dead of night
From forth dull sleep by dreadful fancy waking,
That thinks she hath beheld some ghastly sprite,
Whose grim aspect sets every joint a-shaking;
What terror 'tis! but she, in worser taking,
  From sleep disturbed, heedfully doth view
  The sight which makes supposed terror true.

Wrapp'd and confounded in a thousand fears,
Like to a new-kill'd bird she trembling lies;
She does not look; yet, winking, there appears
Quick-shifting antics, ugly in her eyes:
Such shadows are the weak brain's forgeries:
  Who, angry that the eyes fly from their lights,
  In darkness haunts them with more dreadful sights.

His hand, that yet remains upon her breast,—
Rude ram, to batter such an ivory wall!—
May feel her heart,—(poor citizen!) distress'd,
Wounding itself to death, rise up and fall,
Beating her bulk, that his hand shakes withal.
  This moves in him more rage, and lesser pity,
  To make the breach, and enter this sweet city.

First, like a trumpet, doth his tongue begin
To sound a parley to his heartless foe;
Who o'er the white sheet peers her whiter chin,
The reason of this rash alarm to know,
Which he by dumb demeanour seeks to show;
    But she with vehement prayers urgeth still
    Under what colour he commits this ill.

Thus he replies: "The colour in thy face,—
That even for anger makes the lily pale,
And the red rose blush at her own disgrace,—
Shall plead for me, and tell my loving tale:
Under that colour am I come to scale
    Thy never-conquer'd fort; the fault is thine,
    For those thine eyes betray thee unto mine.

"Thus I forestall thee, if thou mean to chide:
Thy beauty hath ensnar'd thee to this night,
Where thou with patience must my will abide;
My will that marks thee for my earth's delight,
Which I to conquer sought with all my might;
    But as reproof and reason beat it dead,
    By thy bright beauty was it newly bred.

"I see what crosses my attempt will bring;
I know what thorns the growing rose defends;
I think the honey guarded with a sting;
All this, beforehand, counsel comprehends:
But will is deaf, and hears no heedful friends;
    Only he hath an eye to gaze on beauty,
    And dotes on what he looks, 'gainst law or duty.

"I have debated, even in my soul,
What wrong, what shame, what sorrow I shall breed;

But nothing can Affection's course control,
Or stop the headlong fury of his speed.
I know repentant tears ensue the deed,
    Reproach, disdain, and deadly enmity;
    Yet strive I to embrace mine infamy."

This said, he shakes aloft his Roman blade,
Which, like a falcon tow'ring in the skies
Coucheth the fowl below with his wings' shade,
Whose crooked beak threats if he mount he dies:
So under his insulting falchion lies
    Harmless Lucretia, marking what he tells,
    With trembling fear, as fowl hear falcon's bells.

"Lucrece," quoth he, "this night I must enjoy thee:
If thou deny, then force must work my way,
For in thy bed I purpose to destroy thee;
That done, some worthless slave of thine I'll slay,
To kill thine honour with thy life's decay;
    And in thy dead arms do I mean to place him,
    Swearing I slew him, seeing thee embrace him.

"So thy surviving husband shall remain
The scornful mark of every open eye;
Thy kinsmen hang their heads at this disdain,
Thy issue blurr'd with nameless bastardy:
And thou, the author of their obloquy,
    Shalt have thy trespass cited up in rhymes,
    And sung by children in succeeding times.

"But if thou yield, I rest thy secret friend:
The fault unknown is as a thought unacted;
A little harm, done to a great good end,
For lawful policy remains enacted.
The poisonous simple sometimes is compacted

In a pure compound; being so applied,
His venom in effect is purified.

"Then, for thy husband and thy children's sake,
Tender my suit: bequeath not to their lot
The shame that from them no device can take,
The blemish that will never be forgot;
Worse than a slavish wipe, or birth-hour's blot:
        For marks descried in men's nativity
        Are nature's faults, not their own infamy."

Here with a cockatrice' dead-killing eye
He rouseth up himself, and makes a pause;
While she, the picture of pure piety,
Like a white hind under the grype's sharp claws,
Pleads, in a wilderness, where are no laws,
        To the rough beast that knows no gentle right,
        Nor aught obeys but his foul appetite.

But when a black-fac'd cloud the world doth threat,
In his dim mist the aspiring mountains hiding,
From earth's dark womb some gentle gust doth get,
Which blows these pitchy vapours from their biding,
Hindering their present fall by this dividing;
        So his unhallow'd haste her words delays,
        And moody Pluto winks while Orpheus plays.

Yet, foul night-waking cat, he doth but dally,
While in his hold-fast foot the weak mouse panteth;
Her sad behaviour feeds his vulture folly,
A swallowing gulf that even in plenty wanteth:
His ear her prayers admits, but his heart granteth
        No penetrable entrance to her plaining:
        Tears harden lust, though marble wear with raining.

Her pity-pleading eyes are sadly fix'd
In the remorseless wrinkles of his face;
Her modest eloquence with sighs is mix'd,
Which to her oratory adds more grace.
She puts the period often from his place,
    And 'midst the sentence so her accent breaks,
    That twice she doth begin ere once she speaks.

She conjures him by high almighty Jove,
By knighthood, gentry, and sweet friendship's oath,
By her untimely tears, her husband's love,
By holy human law, and common troth,
By heaven and earth, and all the power of both,
    That to his borrow'd bed he make retire,
    And stoop to honour, not to foul desire.

Quoth she, "Reward not hospitality
With such black payment as thou hast pretended;
Mud not the fountain that gave drink to thee;
Mar not the thing that cannot be amended;
End thy ill aim before thy shoot be ended:
    He is no wood-man that doth bend his bow
    To strike a poor unseasonable doe.

"My husband is thy friend,—for his sake spare me;
Thyself art mighty,—for thine own sake leave me;
Myself a weakling,—do not, then, ensnare me;
Thou look'st not like deceit,—do not deceive me.
My sighs, like whirlwinds, labour hence to heave thee:
    If ever man were mov'd with woman's moans,
    Be moved with my tears, my sighs, my groans:

"All which together, like a troubled ocean,
Beat at thy rocky and wreck-threatening heart,

To soften it with their continual motion;
For stones dissolv'd to water do convert.
O, if no harder than a stone thou art,
    Melt at my tears, and be compassionate!
    Soft pity enters at an iron gate.

"In Tarquin's likeness I did entertain thee;
Hast thou put on his shape to do him shame?
To all the host of heaven I complain me,
Thou wrong'st his honour, wound'st his princely name.
Thou art not what thou seem'st; and if the same,
    Thou seem'st not what thou art, a god, a king;
    For kings like gods should govern everything.

"How will thy shame be seeded in thine age,
When thus thy vices bud before thy spring!
If in thy hope thou dar'st do such outrage,
What dar'st thou not when once thou art a king?
O, be remember'd, no outrageous thing
    From vassal actors can be wip'd away;
    Then kings' misdeeds cannot be hid in clay.

"This deed will make thee only lov'd for fear;
But happy monarchs still are fear'd for love:
With foul offenders thou perforce must bear,
When they in thee the like offences prove:
If but for fear of this, thy will remove;
    For princes are the glass, the school, the book,
    Where subjects' eyes do learn, do read, do look.

"And wilt thou be the school when Lust shall learn?
Must he in thee read lectures of such shame?
Wilt thou be glass wherein it shall discern
Authority for sin, warrant for blame?
To privilege dishonour in thy name,

Thou back'st reproach against long-living laud,
And mak'st fair reputation but a bawd.

"Hast thou command? by him that gave it thee,
From a pure heart command thy rebel will:
Draw not thy sword to guard iniquity,
For it was lent thee all that brood to kill.
Thy princely office how canst thou fulfil,
  When, pattern'd by thy fault, foul Sin may say,
  He learn'd to sin, and thou didst teach the way?

"Think but how vile a spectacle it were,
To view thy present trespass in another.
Men's faults do seldom to themselves appear;
Their own transgressions partially they smother:
This guilt would seem death-worthy in thy brother.
  O, how are they wrapp'd in with infamies,
  That from their own misdeeds askance their eyes!

"To thee, to thee, my heav'd-up hands appeal,
Not to seducing lust, thy rash relier;
I sue for exil'd majesty's repeal;
Let him return, and flattering thoughts retire:
His true respect will prison false desire,
  And wipe the dim mist from thy doting eyne,
  That thou shalt see thy state, and pity mine."

"Have done," quoth he; "my uncontrolled tide
Turns not, but swells the higher by this let.
Small lights are soon blown out, huge fires abide,
And with the wind in greater fury fret:
The petty streams that pay a daily debt
  To their salt sovereign, with their fresh falls' haste,
  Add to his flow, but alter not his taste."

"Thou art," quoth she, "a sea, a sovereign king;
And lo, there falls into thy boundless flood
Black lust, dishonour, shame, misgoverning,
Who seek to stain the ocean of thy blood.
If all these petty ills shall change thy good,
     Thy sea within a puddle's womb is hears'd,
     And not the puddle in thy sea dispers'd.

"So shall these slaves be king, and thou their slave;
Thou nobly base, they basely dignified;
Thou their fair life, and they thy fouler grave;
Thou loathed in their shame, they in thy pride:
The lesser thing should not the greater hide;
     The cedar stoops not to the base shrub's foot,
     But low shrubs wither at the cedar's root.

"So let thy thoughts, low vassals to thy state"—
"No more," quoth he, "by heaven, I will not hear thee!
Yield to my love; if not, enforced hate,
Instead of love's coy touch, shall rudely tear thee;
That done, despitefully I mean to bear thee
     Unto the base bed of some rascal groom,
     To by thy partner in this shameful doom."

This said, he sets his foot upon the light,
For light and lust are deadly enemies:
Shame folded up in blind-concealing night,
When most unseen, then most doth tyrannize.
The wolf hath seiz'd his prey, the poor lamb cries;
     Till with her own white fleece her voice controll'd
     Entombs her outcry in her lips' sweet fold:

For with the nightly linen that she wears
He pens her piteous clamours in her head;

Cooling his hot face in the chastest tears
That ever modest eyes with sorrow shed.
O, that prone lust should stain so pure a bed!
 The spots whereof could weeping purify,
 Her tears should drop on them perpetually.

But she hath lost a dearer thing than life,
And he hath won what he would lose again:
This forced league doth force a further strife;
This momentary joy breeds months of pain;
This hot desire converts to cold disdain:
 Pure Chastity is rifled of her store,
 And Lust, the thief, far poorer than before.

Look, as the full-fed hound or gorged hawk,
Unapt for tender smell or speedy flight,
Make slow pursuit, or altogether balk
The prey wherein by nature they delight;
So surfeit-taking Tarquin fares this night:
 His taste delicious, in digestion souring,
 Devours his will, that liv'd by foul devouring.

O, deeper sin than bottomless conceit
Can comprehend in still imagination!
Drunken Desire must vomit his receipt,
Ere he can see his own abomination.
While Lust is in his pride, no exclamation
 Can curb his head, or rein his rash desire,
 Till, like a jade, Self-will himself doth tire.

And then with lank and lean discolour'd cheek,
With heavy eye, knit brow, and strengthless pace,
Feeble Desire, all recreant, poor, and meek,
Like to a bankrupt begger wails his case:
The flesh being proud, Desire doth fight with Grace,

> For there it revels; and when that decays,
> The guilty rebel for remission prays.

So fares it with this faultful lord of Rome,
Who this accomplishment so hotly chas'd;
For now against himself he sounds this doom,—
That through the length of time he stands disgrac'd:
Besides, his soul's fair temple is defac'd;
> To whose weak ruins muster troops of cares,
> To ask the spotted princess how she fares.

She says, her subjects with foul insurrection
Have batter'd down her consecrated wall,
And by their mortal fault brought in subjection
Her immortality, and made her thrall
To living death and pain perpetual:
> Which in her prescience she controlled still,
> But her foresight could not forestall their will.

Even in this thought through the dark night he stealeth,
A captive victor that hath lost in gain;
Bearing away the wound that nothing healeth,
The scar that will, despite of cure, remain;
Leaving his spoil perplex'd in greater pain.
> She bears the load of lust he left behind,
> And he the burden of a guilty mind.

He like a thievish dog creeps sadly thence;
She like a wearied lamb lies panting there;
He scowls, and hates himself for his offence;
She, desperate, with her nails her flesh doth tear;
He faintly flies, sweating with guilty fear;
> She stays, exclaiming on the direful night;
> He runs, and chides his vanish'd, loath'd delight.

He thence departs a heavy convertite;
She there remains a hopeless cast-away;
He in his speed looks for the morning light;
She prays she never may behold the day;
"For day," quoth she, "night's scapes doth open lay,
        And my true eyes have never practis'd how
        To cloak offences with a cunning brow.

"They think not but that every eye can see
The same disgrace which they themselves behold;
And therefore would they still in darkness be,
To have their unseen sin remain untold;
For they their guilt with weeping will unfold,
        And grave, like water, that doth eat in steel,
        Upon my cheeks what helpless shame I feel."

Here she exclaims against repose and rest,
And bids her eyes hereafter still be blind.
She wakes her heart by beating on her breast,
And bids it leap from thence, where it may find
Some purer chest to close so pure a mind.
        Frantic with grief, thus breathes she forth her spite
        Against the unseen secrecy of night:

"O comfort-killing Night, image of hell!
Dim register and notary of shame!
Black stage for tragedies and murders fell!
Vast sin-concealing chaos! nurse of blame!
Blind muffled bawd! dark harbour for defame!
        Grim cave of death! whispering conspirator
        With close-tongu'd treason and the ravisher!

"O, hateful, vaporous, and foggy Night!
Since thou art guilty of my cureless crime,

Muster thy mists to meet the eastern light,
Make war against proportion'd course of time;
Or if thou wilt permit the sun to climb
    His wonted height, yet ere he go to bed,
    Knit poisonous clouds about his golden head.

"With rotten damps ravish the morning air;
Let their exhal'd unwholesome breaths make sick
The life of purity, the supreme fair,
Ere he arrive his weary noon-tide prick;
And let thy misty vapours march so thick,
    That in their smoky ranks his smother'd light
    May set at noon, and make perpetual night.

"Were Tarquin Night (as he is but Night's child),
The silver-shining queen he would distain;
Her twinkling handmaids too, by him defil'd,
Through Night's black bosom should not peep again:
So should I have copartners in my pain;
    And fellowship in woe doth woe assuage,
    As palmers' chat makes short their pilgrimage.

"Where now I have no one to blush with me,
To cross their arms, and hang their heads with mine,
To mask their brows, and hide their infamy;
But I alone must sit and pine,
Seasoning the earth with showers of silver brine,
    Mingling my talk with tears, my grief with groans,
    Poor wasting monuments of lasting moans.

"O Night, thou furnace of foul-reeking smoke,
Let not the jealous Day behold that face
Which underneath thy black all-hiding cloak
Immodestly lies martyr'd with disgrace!
Keep still possession of thy gloomy place,

That all the faults which in thy reign are made
May likewise be sepúlchred in thy shade!

"Make me not object to the tell-tale Day!
The light will show, charácter'd in my brow,
The story of sweet chastity's decay,
The impious breach of holy wedlock vow:
Yea, the illiterate, that know not how
    To 'cipher what is writ in learned books,
    Will quote my loathsome trespass in my looks.

"The nurse, to still her child, will tell my story,
And fright her crying babe with Tarquin's name;
The orator, to deck his oratory,
Will couple my reproach to Tarquin's shame;
Feast-finding minstrels, tuning my defame,
    Will tie the hearers to attend each line,
    How Tarquin wronged me, I Collatine.

"Let my good name, that senseless reputation,
For Collatine's dear love be kept unspotted:
If that be made a theme for disputation,
The branches of another root are rotted,
And undeserv'd reproach to him allotted
    That is as clear from this attaint of mine,
    As I, ere this, was pure to Collatine.

"O unseen shame! invisible disgrace!
O unfelt sore! crest-wounding, private scar!
Reproach is stamp'd in Collatinus' face,
And Tarquin's eye may read the mot afar,
How he in peace is wounded, not in war.
    Alas, how many bear such shameful blows,
    Which not themselves, but he that gives them knows!

"If, Collatine, thine honour lay in me,
From me by strong assault it is bereft.
My honey lost, and I, a drone-like bee,
Have no perfection of my summer left,
But robb'd and ransack'd by injurious theft:
    In thy weak hive a wandering wasp hath crept,
    And suck'd the honey which thy chaste bee kept.

"Yet am I guilty of thy honour's wrack,—
Yet for thy honour did I entertain him;
Coming from thee, I could not push him back,
For it had been dishonour to disdain him:
Besides, of weariness he did complain him,
    And talk'd of virtue;—O, unlook'd-for evil,
    When virtue is profan'd in such a devil!

"Why should the worm intrude the maiden bud?
Or hateful cuckoos hatch in sparrows' nests?
Or toads infect fair founts with venom mud?
Or tyrant folly lurk in gentle breasts?
Or kings be breakers of their own behests?
    But no perfection is so absolute,
    That some impurity doth not pollute.

"The aged man that coffers-up his gold
Is plagu'd with cramps, and gouts and painful fits;
And scarce hath eyes his treasure to behold,
But like still-pining Tantalus he sits,
And useless barns the harvest of his wits;
    Having no other pleasure of his gain
    But torment that it cannot cure his pain.

"So then he hath it, when he cannot use it,
And leaves it to be master'd by his young,

Who in their pride so presently abuse it:
Their father was too weak, and they too strong,
To hold their cursed-blessed fortune long.
    The sweets we wish for turn to loathed sours,
    Even in the moment that we call them ours.

"Unruly blasts wait on the tender spring;
Unwholesome weeds take root with precious flowers;
The adder hisses where the sweet birds sing;
What virtue breeds iniquity devours:
We have no good that we can say is ours,
    But ill-annexed Opportunity
    Or kills his life or else his quality.

"O Opportunity, thy guilt is great!
'Tis thou that execut'st the traitor's treason;
Thou sett'st the wolf where he the lamb may get;
Whoever plots the sin, thou 'point'st the season;
'Tis thou that spurn'st at right, at law, at reason;
    And in thy shady cell, where none may spy him,
    Sits Sin, to seize the souls that wander by him.

"Thou mak'st the vestal violate her oath;
Thou blow'st the fire when temperance is thaw'd;
Thou smother'st honesty, thou murder'st troth;
Thou foul abettor! thou notorious bawd!
Thou plantest scandal, and displacest laud:
    Thou ravisher, thou traitor, thou false thief,
    Thy honey turns to gall, thy joy to grief!

"Thy secret pleasure turns to open shame,
Thy private feasting to a public fast,
Thy smoothing titles to a ragged name;
Thy sugar'd tongue to bitter wormwood taste:
Thy violent vanities can never last.

How comes it, then, vile Opportunity,
Being so bad, such numbers seek for thee?

"When wilt thou be the humble suppliant's friend,
And bring him where his suit may be obtain'd?
When wilt thou sort an hour great strifes to end?
Or free that soul which wretchedness hath chain'd?
Give physic to the sick, ease to the pain'd
    The poor, lame, blind, halt, creep, cry out for thee;
    But they ne'er meet with Opportunity.

"The patient dies while the physician sleeps;
The orphan pines while the oppressor feeds;
Justice is feasting while the widow weeps;
Advice is sporting while infection breeds;
Thou grant'st no time for charitable deeds;
    Wrath, envy, treason, rape, and murder's rages,
    Thy heinous hours wait on them as their pages.

"When Truth and Virtue have to do with thee
A thousand crosses keep them from thy aid:
They buy the help; but Sin ne'er gives a fee,
He gratis comes; and thou art well appaid
As well to hear as grant what he hath said.
    My Collatine would else have come to me
    When Tarquin did, but he was stay'd by thee.

"Guilty thou art of murder and of theft;
Guilty of perjury and subornation;
Guilty of treason, forgery, and shift;
Guilty of incest, that abomination:
An accessary by thine inclination
    To all sins past, and all that are to come,
    From the creation to the general doom.

"Mis-shapen Time, copesmate of ugly Night,
Swift-subtle post, carrier of grisly care,
Eater of youth, false slave to false delight,
Base watch of woes, sin's pack-horse, virtue's snare;
Thou nursest all, and murder'st all that are:
  O, hear me, then, injurious-shifting Time!
  Be guilty of my death, since of my crime.

"Why hath thy servant, Opportunity,
Betray'd the hours thou gav'st me to repose?
Cancell'd my fortunes, and enchained me
To endless date of never-ending woes?
Time's office is to fine the hate of foes;
  To eat up errors by opinion bred,
  Not spend the dowry of a lawful bed.

"Time's glory is to calm contending kings,
To unmask falsehood, and bring truth to light,
To stamp the seal of time in aged things,
To wake the morn, and sentinel the night,
To wrong the wronger till he render right,
  To ruinate proud buildings with thy hours,
  And smear with dust their glittering-golden towers;

"To fill with worm-holes stately monuments,
To feed oblivion with decay of things,
To blot old books and alter their contents,
To pluck the quills from ancient ravens' wings,
To dry the old oak's sap, and cherish springs,
  To spoil antiquities of hammer'd steel,
  And turn the giddy round of Fortune's wheel;

"To show the beldame daughters of her daughter,
To make the child a man, the man a child,

To slay the tiger that doth live by slaughter,
To tame the unicorn and lion wild,
To mock the subtle in themselves beguil'd;
    To cheer the ploughman with increaseful crops,
    And waste huge stones with little water-drops.

"Why work'st thou mischief in thy pilgrimage,
Unless thou couldst return to make amends?
One poor retiring minute in an age
Would purchase thee a thousand-thousand friends,
Lending him wit that to bad debtors lends:
    O, this dread night, wouldst thou one hour come back,
    I could prevent this storm, and shun thy wrack!

"Thou ceaseless lackey to eternity,
With some mischance cross Tarquin in his flight:
Devise extremes beyond extremity,
To make him curse this cursed crimeful night:
Let ghastly shadows his lewd eyes affright;
    And the dire thought of his committed evil
    Shape every bush a hideous-shapeless devil.

"Disturb his hours of rest with restless trances,
Afflict him in his bed with bedrid groans;
Let there bechance him pitiful mischances,
To make him moan, but pity not his moans:
Stone him with harden'd hearts, harder than stones;
    And let mild women to him lose their mildness,
    Wilder to him than tigers in their wildness.

"Let him have time to tear his curled hair,
Let him have time against himself to rave,
Let him have time of Time's help to despair,
Let him have time to live a loathed slave,
Let him have time a beggar's orts to crave;

And time to see one that by alms doth live
Disdain to him disdained scraps to give.

"Let him have time to see his friends his foes,
And merry fools to mock at him resort;
Let him have time to mark how slow time goes
In time of sorrow, and how swift and short
His time of folly and his time of sport;
    And ever let his unrecalling crime
    Have time to wail th' abusing of his time.

"O Time, thou tutor both to good and bad,
Teach me to curse him that thou taught'st this ill!
At his own shadow let the thief run mad,
Himself himself seek every hour to kill!
Such wretched hands such wretched blood should spill;
    For who so base would such an office have
    As slanderous death's-man to so base a slave?

"The baser is he, coming from a king,
To shame his hope with deeds degenerate:
The mightier man, the mightier is the thing
That makes him honour'd, or begets him hate;
For greatest scandal waits on greatest state.
    The moon being clouded presently is miss'd,
    But little stars may hide them when they list.

"The crow may bathe his coal-black wings in mire,
And unperceiv'd fly with the filth away;
But if the like the snow-white swan desire,
The stain upon his silver down will stay.
Poor grooms are sightless night, kings glorious day.
    Gnats are unnoted wheresoe'er they fly,
    But eagles gaz'd upon with every eye.

"Out, idle words, servants to shallow fools!
Unprofitable sounds, weak arbitrators!
Busy yourselves in skill-contending schools,
Debate where leisure serves with dull debaters;
To trembling clients be you mediators:
    For me, I force not argument a straw,
    Since that my case is past the help of law.

"In vain I rail at Opportunity,
At Time, at Tarquin, and uncheerful Night;
In vain I cavil with my infamy,
In vain I spurn at my confirm'd despite:
This helpless smoke of words doth me no right.
    This remedy indeed to do me good,
    Is to let forth my foul-defiled blood.

"Poor hand, why quiver'st thou at this decree?
Honour thyself to rid me of this shame;
For if I die, my honour lives in thee;
But if I live, thou liv'st in my defame:
Since thou couldst not defend thy loyal dame,
    And wast afear'd to scratch her wicked foe,
    Kill both thyself and her for yielding so."

This said, from her be-tumbled couch she starteth,
To find some desperate instrument of death:
But this no-slaughter-house no tool imparteth,
To make more vent for passage of her breath,
Which, thronging through her lips, so vanisheth
    As smoke from Ætna, that in air consumes,
    Or that which from discharged cannon fumes.

"In vain," quoth she, "I live, and seek in vain
Some happy mean to end a hapless life.

I fear'd by Tarquin's falchion to be slain,
Yet for the self-same purpose seek a knife:
But when I fear'd I was a loyal wife:
    So am I now:—O no, that cannot be;
    Of that true type hath Tarquin rifled me!

"O, that is gone for which I sought to live,
And therefore now I need not fear to die.
To clear this spot by death, at least I give
A badge of fame to slander's livery;
A dying life to living infamy:
    Poor helpless help, the treasure stol'n away,
    To burn the guiltless casket where it lay!

"Well, well, dear Collatine, thou shalt not know
The stained taste of violated troth;
I will not wrong thy true affection so,
To flatter thee with an infringed oath;
This bastard graff shall never come to growth:
    He shall not boast who did thy stock pollute
    That thou art doting father of his fruit.

"Nor shall he smile at thee in secret thought,
Nor laugh with his companions at thy state;
But thou shalt know thy interest was not bought
Basely with gold, but stol'n from forth thy gate.
For me, I am the mistress of my fate,
    And with my trespass never will dispense,
    Till life to death acquit my forc'd offence.

"I will not poison thee with my attaint,
Nor fold my fault in cleanly-coin'd excuses;
My sable ground of sin I will not paint,
To hide the truth of this false night's abuses:
My tongue shall utter all; mine eyes like sluices,

As from a mountain-spring that feeds a dale,
Shall gush pure streams to purge my impure tale."

By this, lamenting Philomel had ended
The well-tun'd warble of her nightly sorrow,
And solemn night with slow-sad gait descended
To ugly hell; when, lo the blushing morrow
Lends light to all fair eyes that light will borrow;
    But cloudy Lucrece shames herself to see,
    And therefore still in night would cloister'd be.

Revealing day through every cranny spies,
And seems to point her out where she sits weeping;
To whom she sobbing speaks: "O, eye of eyes,
Why pry'st thou through my window? leave thy peeping;
Mock with thy tickling beams eyes that are sleeping;
    Brand not my forehead with thy piercing light,
    For day hath nought to do what's done by night."

Thus cavils she with everything she sees:
True grief is fond and testy as a child,
Who wayward once, his mood with nought agrees.
Old woes, not infant sorrows, bear them mild;
Continuance tames the one; the other wild,
    Like an unpractis'd swimmer plunging still,
    With too much labour drowns for want of skill.

So she, deep-drenched in a sea of care,
Holds disputation with each thing she views,
And to herself all sorrow doth compare;
No object but her passion's strength renews;
And as one shifts, another straight ensues:
    Sometime her grief is dumb, and hath no words;
    Sometime 'tis mad, and too much talk affords.

The little birds that tune their morning's joy
Make her moans mad with their sweet melody:
For mirth doth search the bottom of annoy;
Sad souls are slain in merry company;
Grief best is pleas'd with grief's society:
    True sorrow then is feelingly suffic'd
    When with like semblance it is sympathiz'd.

'Tis double death to drown in ken of shore;
He ten times pines that pines beholding food;
To see the salve doth make the wound ache more;
Great grief grieves most at that would do it good;
Deep woes roll forward like a gentle flood,
    Who, being stopp'd, the bounding banks o'erflows;
    Grief dallied with nor law nor limit knows.

"You mocking birds," quoth she, "your tunes entomb
Within your hollow-swelling feather'd breasts,
And in my hearing be you mute and dumb!
My restless discord loves no stops nor rests;
A woeful hostess brooks not merry guests:
    Relish your nimble notes to pleasing ears;
    Distress likes dumps when time is kept with tears.

"Come, Philomel, that sing'st of ravishment,
Make thy sad grove in my dishevell'd hair:
As the dank earth weeps at thy languishment,
So I at each sad strain will strain a tear,
And with deep groans the diapason bear;
    For burden-wise I'll hum on Tarquin still,
    While thou on Tereus descant'st better still.

"And whiles against a thorn thou bear'st thy part,
To keep thy sharp woes waking, wretched I,

To imitate thee well, against my heart
Will fix a sharp knife, to affright mine eye;
Who, if it wink, shall thereon fall and die.
    These means, as frets upon an instrument,
    Shall tune our heart-strings to true languishment.

"And for, poor bird, thou sing'st not in the day,
As shaming any eye should thee behold,
Some dark-deep desert, seated from the way,
That knows not parching heat nor freezing cold,
We will find out; and there we will unfold
    To creatures stern sad tunes, to change their kinds:
    Since men prove beasts let beasts bear gentle minds."

As the poor frightened deer, that stands at gaze,
Wildly determining which way to fly,
Or one encompass'd with a winding maze,
That cannot tread the way out readily;
So with herself is she in mutiny,
    To live or die which of the twain were better.
    When life is sham'd, and death reproach's debtor.

"To kill myself," quoth she, "alack! what were it,
But with my body my poor soul's pollution?
They that lose half with greater patience bear it
Than they whose whole is swallowed in confusion.
That mother tries a merciless conclusion
    Who, having two sweet babes, when death takes one,
    Will slay the other, and be nurse to none.

"My body or my soul, which was the dearer,
When the one pure, the other made divine?
Whose love of either to myself was nearer,
When both were kept for heaven and Collatine?
Ay me! the bark peel'd from the lofty pine,

His leaves will wither, and his sap decay;
So must my soul, her bark being peel'd away.

"Her house is sack'd, her quiet interrupted,
Her mansion batter'd by the enemy;
Her sacred temple spotted, spoil'd, corrupted,
Grossly engirt with daring infamy:
Then let it not be call'd impiety,
　　If in this blemish'd fort I make some hole
　　Through which I may convey this troubled soul.

"Yet die I will not till my Collatine
Have heard the cause of my untimely death;
That he may vow, in that sad hour of mine,
Revenge on him that made me stop my breath.
My stained blood to Tarquin I'll bequeath,
　　Which by him tainted shall for him be spent,
　　And as his due, writ in my testament.

"My honour I'll bequeath unto the knife
That wounds my body so dishonoured.
'Tis honour to deprive dishonour'd life;
The one will live, the other being dead:
So of shame's ashes shall my fame be bred;
　　For in my death I murder shameful scorn:
　　My shame so dead, mine honour is new-born.

"Dear lord of that dear jewel I have lost,
What legacy shall I bequeath to thee?
My resolution, love, shall be thy boast,
By whose example thou reveng'd mayst be.
How Tarquin must be us'd, read it in me:
　　Myself, thy friend, will kill myself, thy foe,
　　And, for my sake, serve thou false Tarquin so.

"This brief abridgment of my will I make:—
My soul and body to the skies and ground;
My resolution, husband, do thou take;
Mine honour be the knife's that makes my wound;
My shame be his that did my fame confound;
    And all my fame that lives disbursed be
    To those that live, and think no shame of me.

"Thou, Collatine, shalt oversee this will;
How I was overseen that thou shalt see it!
My blood shall wash the slander of mine ill;
My life's foul deed, my life's fair end shall free it.
Faint not, faint heart, but stoutly say, 'So be it.'
    Yield to my hand; my hand shall conquer thee:
    Thou dead, both die, and both shall victors be."

This plot of death when sadly she had laid,
And wip'd the brinish pearl from her bright eyes,
With untun'd tongue she hoarsely call'd her maid,
Whose swift obedience to her mistress hies;
For fleet-wing'd duty with thought's feathers flies.
    Poor Lucrece' cheeks unto her maid seem so
    As winter meads when sun doth melt their snow.

Her mistress she doth give demure good-morrow,
With soft-slow tongue, true mark of modesty,
And sorts a sad look to her lady's sorrow,
For why her face wore sorrow's livery;
But durst not ask of her audaciously
    Why her two suns were cloud-eclipsed so,
    Now why her fair cheeks over-wash'd with woe.

But as the earth doth weep, the sun being set,
Each flower moisten'd like a melting eye;

Even so the maid with swelling drops 'gan wet
Her circled eyne, enforc'd by sympathy
Of those fair suns set in her mistress' sky,
    Who in a salt-wav'd ocean quenched their light,
    Which makes the maid weep like the dewy night.

A pretty while these pretty creatures stand,
Like ivory conduits coral cisterns filling:
One justly weeps; the other takes in hand
No cause, but company, of her drops spilling:
Their gentle sex to weep are often willing;
    Grieving themselves to guess at others' smarts,
    And then they drown their eyes, or break their hearts.

For men have marble, women waxen, minds,
And therefore are they form'd as marble will;
The weak oppress'd, the impression of strange kinds
Is form'd in them by force, by fraud, or skill:
Then call them not the authors of their ill,
    No more than wax shall be accounted evil,
    Wherein is stamp'd the semblance of a devil.

Their smoothness, like a goodly champaign plain,
Lays open all the little worms that creep;
In men, as in a rough-grown grove, remain
Cave-keeping evils that obscurely sleep:
Through crystal walls each little mote will peep:
    Though men can cover crimes with bold stern looks,
    Poor women's faces are their own faults' books.

No man inveigh against the wither'd flower,
But chide rough winter that the flower hath kill'd:
Not that devour'd, but that which doth devour,
Is worthy blame. O, let it not be hild
Poor women's faults that they are so fulfill'd

With men's abuses! those proud lords, to blame,
Make weak-made women tenants to their shame.

The precedent whereof in Lucrece' view,
Assail'd by night with circumstances strong
Of present death, and shame that might ensue
By that her death, to do her husband wrong:
Such danger to resistance did belong,
    That dying fear through all her body spread;
    And who cannot abuse a body dead?

By this, mild patience bid fair Lucrece speak
To the poor counterfeit of her complaining:
"My girl," quoth she, "on what occasion break
Those tears from thee, that down thy cheeks are raining?
If thou dost weep for grief of my sustaining,
    Know, gentle wench, it small avails my mood:
    If tears could help, mine own would do me good.

"But tell me, girl, when went"—and there she stay'd
Till after a deep groan—"Tarquin from hence?"
"Madam, ere I was up," replied the maid,
"The more to blame my sluggard negligence:
Yet with the fault I thus far can dispense,—
    Myself was stirring ere the break of day,
    And, ere I rose, was Tarquin gone away.

"But lady, if your maid may be so bold,
She would request to know your heaviness."
"O, peace!" quoth Lucrece; "if it should be told,
The repetition cannot make it less;
For more it is than I can well express:
    And that deep torture may be call'd a hell,
    When more is felt than one hath power to tell.

"Go, get me hither paper, ink, and pen,—
Yet save that labour, for I have them here.
What should I say?—One of my husband's men
Bid thou be ready, by and by, to bear
A letter to my lord, my love, my dear:
    Bid him with speed prepare to carry it;
    The cause craves haste, and it will soon be writ."

Her maid is gone, and she prepares to write,
First hovering o'er the paper with her quill:
Conceit and grief an eager combat fight;
What wit sets down is blotted straight with will;
This is too curious-good, this blunt and ill:
    Much like a press of people at a door,
    Throng her inventions, which shall go before.

At last she thus begins:—"Thou worthy lord
Of that unworthy wife that greeteth thee,
Health to thy person! next vouchsafe t' afford
(If ever, love, thy Lucrece thou wilt see)
Some present speed to come and visit me.
    So I commend me from our house in grief:
    My woes are tedious, though my words are brief."

Here she folds up the tenour of her woe,
Her certain sorrow writ uncertainly.
By this short schedule Collatine may know
Her grief, but not her grief's true quality;
She dares not thereof make discovery,
    Lest he should hold it her own gross abuse,
    Ere she with blood had stain'd her stain'd excuse.

Besides, the life and feeling of her passion
She hoards, to spend when he is by to hear her;

When signs and groans and tears may grace the fashion
Of her disgrace, the better so to clear her
From that suspicion which the world might bear her.
    To shun this blot, she would not blot the letter
    With words, till action might become them better.

To see sad sights moves more than hear them told;
For then the eye interprets to the ear
The heavy motion that it doth behold:
When every part a part of woe doth bear,
'Tis but a part of sorrow that we hear:
    Deep sounds make lesser noise than shallow fords,
    And sorrow ebbs, being blown with wind of words.

Her letter now is seal'd, and on it writ,
"At Ardea to my lord with more than haste."
The post attends, and she delivers it,
Charging the sour-fac'd groom to hie as fast
As lagging fowls before the northern blast:
    Speed more than speed but dull and slow she deems:
    Extremity still urgeth such extremes.

The homely villain court'sies to her low;
And, blushing on her, with a steadfast eye
Receives the scroll without or yea or no,
And forth with bashful innocence doth hie.
But they whose guilt within their bosoms lie
    Imagine every eye beholds their blame;
    For Lucrece thought he blush'd to see her shame:

When, silly groom! God wot, it was defect
Of spirit, life, and bold audacity.
Such harmless creatures have a true respect
To talk in deeds, while others saucily
Promise more speed, but do it leisurely:

Even so this pattern of the worn-out age
Pawn'd honest looks, but laid no words to gage.

His kindled duty kindled her mistrust
That two red fires in both their faces blaz'd;
She thought he blush'd, as knowing Tarquin's lust,
And, blushing with him, wistly on him gaz'd;
Her earnest eye did make him more amaz'd:
    The more she saw the blood his cheeks replenish,
    The more she thought he spied in her some blemish.

But long she thinks till he return again,
And yet the duteous vassal scarce is gone.
The weary time she cannot entertain,
For now 'tis stale to sigh, to weep, and groan:
So woe hath wearied woe, moan tired moan,
    That she plaints a little while doth stay,
    Pausing for means to mourn some newer way.

At last she calls to mind where hangs a piece
Of skilful painting, made for Priam's Troy;
Before the which is drawn the power of Greece,
For Helen's rape the city to destroy,
Threat'ning cloud-kissing Ilion with annoy;
    Which the conceited painter drew so proud,
    As heaven, it seem'd, to kiss the turrets bow'd.

A thousand lamentable objects there,
In scorn of nature, art gave lifeless life:
Many a dry drop seem'd a weeping tear,
Shed for the slaughter'd husband by the wife:
The red blood reek'd to show the painter's strife;
    And dying eyes gleam'd forth their ashy lights,
    Like dying coals burnt out in tedious nights.

There might you see the labouring pioneer
Begrim'd with sweat, and smeared all with dust;
And from the towers of Troy there would appear
The very eyes of men through loop-holes thrust,
Gazing upon the Greeks with little lust:
 Such a sweet observance in this work was had,
 That one might see those far-off eyes look sad.

In great commanders grace and majesty
You might behold, triúmphing in their faces;
In youth, quick bearing and detexerity;
And here and there the painter interlaces
Pale cowards, marching on with trembling paces
 Which heartless peasants did so well resemble,
 That one would swear he saw them quake and tremble.

In Ajax and Ulysses, O, what art
Of physiognomy might one behold!
The face of either 'cipher'd either's heart;
Their face their manners most expressly told:
In Ajax' eyes blunt rage and rigour roll'd;
 But the mild glance that sly Ulysses lent,
 Show'd deep regard and smiling government.

There pleading might you see grave Nestor stand,
As 't were encouraging the Greeks to fight;
Making such sober action with his hand
That it beguil'd attention, charm'd the sight:
In speech, it seem'd, his beard all silver white
 Wagg'd up and down, and from his lips did fly
 Thin winding breath, which purl'd up to the sky.

About him were a press of gaping faces,
Which seem'd to swallow up his sound advice;

All jointly listening, but with several graces,
As if some mermaid did their ears entice;
Some high, some low; the painter was so nice,
    The scalps of many, almost hid behind,
    To jump up higher seem'd, to mock the mind.

Here one man's hand lean'd on another's head,
His nose being shadow'd by his neighbour's ear;
Here one, being throng'd, bears back, all boll'n and red;
Another, smother'd, seems to pelt and swear;
And in their rage such signs of rage they bear,
    As, but for loss of Nestor's golden words,
    It seem'd they would debate with angry swords.

For much imaginary work was there;
Conceit deceitful, so compact, so kind,
That for Achilles' image stood his spear,
Grip'd in an armed hand; himself, behind,
Was left unseen, save to the eye of mind:
    A hand, a foot, a face, a leg, a head,
    Stood for the whole to be imagined.

And from the walls of strong-besieged Troy
When their brave hope, bold Hector, march'd to field,
Stood many Trojan mothers, sharing joy
To see their youthful sons bright weapons wield;
And to their hope they such odd action yield,
    That through their light joy seemed to appear
    (Like bright things stain'd) a kind of heavy fear.

And from the strand of Dardan, where they fought,
To Simois' reedy banks the red blood ran,
Whose waves to imitate the battle sought
With swelling ridges; and their ranks began
To break upon the galled shore, and than

Retire again, till, meeting greater ranks,
They join, and shoot their foam at Simois' banks.

To this well-painted piece is Lucrece come,
To find a face where all distress is stell'd.
Many she sees where cares have carved some,
But none where all distress and dolour dwell'd,
Till she despairing Hecuba beheld,
    Staring on Priam's wounds with her old eyes,
    Which bleeding under Pyrrhus' proud foot lies.

In her the painter had anatomiz'd
Time's ruin, beauty's wreck, and grim care's reign:
Her cheeks with chaps and wrinkles were disguis'd;
Of what she was no semblance did remain:
Her blue blood chang'd to black in every vein,
    Wanting the spring that those shrunk pipes had fed,
    Show'd life imprison'd in a body dead.

On this sad shadow Lucrece spends her eyes,
And shapes her sorrow to the beldam's woes,
Who nothing wants to answer her but cries,
And bitter words to ban her cruel foes:
The painter was no god to lend her those;
    And therefore Lucrece swears he did her wrong,
    To give her so much grief, and not a tongue.

"Poor instrument," quoth she, "without a sound,
I'll tune thy woes with my lamenting tongue;
And drop sweet balm in Priam's painted wound,
And rail on Pyrrhus that hath done him wrong;
And with my tears quench Troy that burns so long;
    And with my knife scratch out the angry eyes
    Of all the Greeks that are thine enemies.

"Show me the strumpet that began this stir,
That with my nails her beauty I may tear.
Thy heat of lust, fond Paris, did incur
This load of wrath that burning Troy doth bear:
Thy eye kindled the fire that burneth here;
    And here in Troy, for trespass of thine eye,
    The sire, the son, the dame, and daughter die.

"Why should the private pleasure of some one
Become the public plague of many mo?
Let sin, alone committed, light alone
Upon his head that hath transgressed so;
Let guiltless souls be freed from guilty woe:
    For one's offence why should so many fall,
    To plague a private sin in general?

"Lo, here weeps Hecuba, here Priam dies,
Here manly Hector faints, here Troilus swounds,
Here friend by friend in bloody channel lies,
And friend to friend gives unadvised wounds,
And one man's lust these many lives confounds:
    Had doting Priam check'd his son's desire,
    Troy had been bright with fame, and not with fire."

Here feelingly she weeps Troy's painted woes:
For sorrow, like a heavy-hanging bell,
Once set on ringing, with his own weight goes;
Then little strength rings out the doleful knell:
So Lucrece, set a-work, sad tales doth tell
    To pencill'd pensiveness and colour'd sorrow;
    She lends them words, and she their looks doth borrow.

She throws her eyes about the painting round,
And whom she finds forlorn she doth lament.

At last she sees a wretched image bound,
That piteous looks to Phrygian shepherds lent;
His face, though full of cares, yet show'd content.
    Onward to Troy with the blunt swains he goes,
    So mild, that Patience seem'd to scorn his woes.

In him the painter labour'd with his skill
To hide deceit, and give the harmless show
A humble gait, calm looks, eyes wailing still,
A brow unbent, that seem'd to welcome woe;
Cheeks neither red nor pale, but mingled so
    That blushing red no guilty instance gave,
    Nor ashy pale the fear that false hearts have.

But, like a constant and confirmed devil,
He entertain'd a show so seeming just,
And therein so ensconc'd his secret evil,
That jealousy itself could not mistrust
False-creeping craft and perjury should thrust
    Into so bright a day such black-fac'd storms,
    Or blot with hell-born sin such saint-like forms.

The well-skill'd workman this mild image drew
For perjured Sinon, whose enchanting story
The credulous old Priam after slew;
Whose words, like wild-fire, burnt the shining glory
Of rich-built Ilion, that the skies were sorry,
    And little stars shot from their fixed places,
    When their glass fell wherein they view'd their faces.

This picture she avisedly perus'd,
And chid the painter for his wondrous skill,
Saying, some shape in Sinon's was abus'd;
So fair a form lodg'd not a mind so ill:
And still on him she gaz'd, and gazing still,

Such signs of truth in his plain face she spied,
That she concludes the picture was belied.

"It cannot be," quoth she, "that so much guile"—
She would have said "can lurk in such a look;"
But Tarquin's shape came in her mind the while,
And from her tongue "can lurk" from "cannot" took:
"It cannot be," she in that sense forsook,
     And turn'd it thus,—"It cannot be, I find,
     But such a face should bear a wicked mind:

"For even as subtle Sinon here is painted,
So sober-sad, so weary, and so mild,
(As if with grief or travail he had fainted)
To me came Tarquin armed; so beguil'd
With outward honesty, but yet defil'd
     With inward vice: as Priam did him cherish,
     So did I Tarquin; so my Troy did perish.

"Look, look, how listening Priam wets his eyes,
To see those borrow'd tears that Sinon sheds!
Priam, why art thou old, and yet not wise?
For every tear he falls a Trojan bleeds:
His eye drops fire, no water thence proceeds;
     Those round clear pearls of his, that move thy pity,
     Are balls of quenchless fire to burn thy city.

"Such devils steal effects from lightless hell;
For Sinon in his fire doth quake with cold,
And in that cold hot-burning fire doth dwell;
These contraries such unity do hold,
Only to flatter fools, and make them bold:
     So Priam's trust false Sinon's tears doth flatter,
     That he finds means to burn his Troy with water."

Here, all enrag'd, such passion her assails,
That patience is quite beaten from her breast.
She tears the senseless Sinon with her nails,
Comparing him to that unhappy guest
Whose deed hath made herself herself detest:
    At last she smilingly with this gives o'er;
    "Fool! fool!" quoth she, "his wounds will not be sore."

Thus ebbs and flows the current of her sorrow,
And time doth weary time with her complaining.
She looks for night, and then she longs for morrow,
And both she thinks too long with her remaining:
Short time seems long in sorrow's sharp sustaining:
    Though woe be heavy, yet it seldom sleeps;
    And they that watch see time how slow it creeps.

Which all this time hath overslipp'd her thought,
That she with painted images hath spent;
Being from the feeling of her own grief brought
By deep surmise of other's detriment;
Losing her woes in shows of discontent.
    It easeth some, though none it ever cur'd,
    To think their dolour others have endur'd.

But now the mindful messenger, come back,
Brings home his lord and other company;
Who finds his Lucrece clad in mourning black;
And round about her tear-distained eye
Blue circles stream'd like rainbows in the sky:
    These water-galls in her dim element
    Foretell new storms to those already spent.

Which when her sad-beholding husband saw,
Amazedly in her sad face he stares:

Her eyes, though sod in tears, look'd red and raw,
Her lively colour kill'd with deadly cares.
He hath no power to ask her how she fares;
    But stood, like old acquaintance in a trance,
    Met far from home, wondering each other's chance.

At last he takes her by the bloodless hand,
And thus begins: "What uncouth ill event
Hath thee befall'n, that thou dost trembling stand?
Sweet love, what spite hath thy fair colour spent?
Why art thou thus attir'd in discontent?
    Unmask, dear-dear, this moody heaviness,
    And tell thy grief, that we may give redress."

Three times with sighs she gives her sorrow fire,
Ere once she can discharge one word of woe:
At length address'd to answer his desire,
She modestly prepares to let them know
Her honour is ta'en prisoner by the foe;
    While Collatine and his consorted lords
    With sad attention long to hear her words.

And now this pale swan in her watery nest
Begins the sad dirge of her certain ending:
"Few words," quoth she, "shall fit the trespass best,
Where no excuse can give the fault amending:
In me more woes than words are now depending;
    And my laments would be drawn out too long,
    To tell them all with one poor tired tongue.

"Then be this all the task it hath to say:—
Dear husband, in the interest of thy bed
A stranger came, and on that pillow lay
Where thou wast wont to rest thy weary head;
And what wrong else may be imagined

By foul enforcement might be done to me,
From that, alas! thy Lucrece is not free.

"For in the dreadful dead of dark midnight,
With shining falchion in my chamber came
A creeping creature, with a flaming light,
And softly cried, 'Awake, thou Roman dame,
And entertain my love; else lasting shame
    On thee and thine this night I will inflict,
    If thou my love's desire do contradict.

"'For some hard-favour'd groom of thine,' quoth he,
'Unless thou yoke thy liking to my will,
I'll murder straight, and then I'll slaughter thee,
And swear I found you where you did fulfil
The loathsome act of lust, and so did kill
    The lechers in their deed: this act will be
    My fame, and thy perpetual infamy.'

"With this, I did begin to start and cry;
And then against my heart he set his sword,
Swearing, unless I took all patiently,
I should not live to speak another word;
So should my shame still rest upon record,
    And never be forgot in mighty Rome
    Th' adulterate death of Lucrece and her groom.

"Mine enemy was strong, my poor self weak,
And far the weaker with so strong a fear:
My bloody judge forbade my tongue to speak;
No rightful plea might plead for justice there:
His scarlet lust came evidence to swear
    That my poor beauty had purloin'd his eyes;
    And when the judge is robb'd, the prisoner dies.

"O, teach me how to make mine own excuse!
Or, at the least, this refuge let me find,—
Though my gross blood be stain'd with this abuse,
Immaculate and spotless in my mind;
That was not forc'd; that never was inclin'd
        To accessory yieldings, but still pure
        Doth in her poison'd closet yet endure."

Lo, here, the hopeless merchant of this loss,
With head declin'd, and voice damn'd up with woe,
With sad-set eyes, and wretched arms across,
From lips new-waxen pale begins to blow
The grief away that stops his answer so:
        But, wretched as he is, he strives in vain;
        What he breathes out his breath drinks up again.

As through an arch the violent-roaring tide
Outruns the eye that doth behold his haste,
Yet in the eddy boundeth in his pride
Back to the strait that forc'd him on so fast;
In rage sent out, recall'd in rage, being past:
        Even so his sighs, his sorrows, make a saw,
        To push grief on, and back the same grief draw.

Which speechless woe of his poor she attendeth,
And his untimely frenzy thus awaketh:
"Dear lord, thy sorrow to my sorrow lendeth
Another power; no flood by raining slaketh.
My woe too sensible thy passion maketh
        More feeling-painful: let it, then, suffice
        To drown one woe, one pair of weeping eyes.

"And for my sake, when I might charm thee so,
For she that was my Lucrece,—not attend me:

Be suddenly revenged upon my foe,
Thine, mine, his own: suppose thou dost defend me
From what is past; the help that thou shalt lend me
    Comes all too late, yet let the traitor die;
    For sparing justice feeds iniquity.

"But ere I name him, you, fair lords," quoth she,
Speaking to those that came with Collatine,
"Shall plight your honourable faiths to me,
With swift pursuit to venge this wrong of mine;
For 'tis a meritorious fair design
    To chase injustice with revengeful arms:
    Knights, by their oaths, should right poor ladies' harms."

At this request, with noble disposition
Each present lord began to promise aid,
As bound in knighthood to her imposition,
Longing to hear the hateful foe bewray'd:
But she, that yet her sad task hath not said,
    The protestation stops. "O, speak," quoth she,
    "How may this forced stain be wip'd from me?

"What is the quality of mine offence?
Being constrain'd with dreadful circumstance,
May my pure mind with the foul act dispense?
My low-declined honour to advance,
May any terms acquit me from this chance?
    The poison'd fountain clears itself again;
    And why not I from this compelled stain?"

With this, they all at once began to say,
Her body's stain her mind untainted clears;
While with a joyless smile she turns away
The face, that map which deep impression bears
Of hard misfortune, carv'd in it with tears.

"No, no," quoth she, "no dame, hereafter living,
By my excuse shall claim excuse's giving."

Here with a sigh, as if her heart would break,
She throws forth Tarquin's name: "He! he!" she says,
But more than "he!" her poor tongue could not speak;
Till after many accents and delays,
Untimely breathings, sick and short assays,
    She utters this, "He, he, fair lords, 'tis he,
    That guides this hand to give this wound to me!"

Even here she sheathed in her harmless breast
A harmful knife, that thence her soul unsheath'd:
That blow did bail it from the deep unrest
Of that polluted prison where it breath'd:
Her contrite sighs unto the clouds bequeath'd
    Her winged sprite, and through her wounds doth fly
    Life's lasting date from cancell'd destiny.

Stone-still astonish'd with this deadly deed,
Stood Collatine and all his lordly crew;
Till Lucrece' father, that beholds her bleed,
Himself on her self-slaughter'd body threw;
And from the purple fountain Brutus drew
    The murderous knife, and, as it left the place,
    Her blood, in poor revenge, held it in chase;

And bubbling from her breast, it doth divide
In two slow rivers, that the crimson blood
Circles her body in on every side,
Who, like a late-sack'd island, vastly stood
Bare and unpeopled in this fearful flood.
    Some of her blood still pure and red remain'd,
    And some look'd black, and that false Tarquin stain'd.

About the mourning and congealed face
Of that black blood a watery rigol goes,
Which seems to weep upon the tainted place:
And ever since, as pitying Lucrece' woes,
Corrupted blood some watery token shows;
  And blood untainted still doth red abide,
  Blushing at that which is so putrified.

"Daughter, dear daughter," old Lucretius cries,
"That life was mine which thou hast here depriv'd.
If in the child the father's image lies,
Where shall I live now Lucrece is unliv'd?
Thou wast not to this end from me deriv'd.
  If children pre-decease progenitors,
  We are their offspring, and they none of ours.

"Poor broken glass, I often did behold
In thy sweet semblance my old age new born;
But now that fair-fresh mirror, dim and old,
Shows me a bare-bon'd death by time outworn:
O, from thy cheeks my image thou hast torn,
  And shiver'd all the beauty of my glass,
  That I no more can see what once I was!

"O time, cease thou thy course, and last no longer,
If they surcease to be that should survive!
Shall rotten death make conquest of the stronger,
And leave the faltering feeble souls alive?
The old bees die, the young possess their hive:
  They live, sweet Lucrece, live again, and see
  Thy father die, and not thy father thee!"

By this, starts Collatine as from a dream,
And bids Lucretius give his sorrow place;

And then in key-cold Lucrece' bleeding stream
He falls, and bathes the pale fear in his face,
And counterfeits to die with her a space;
    Till manly shame bids him possess his breath,
    And live to be revenged on her death.

The deep vexation of his inward soul
Hath serv'd a dumb arrest upon his tongue;
Who, mad that sorrow should his use control,
Or keep him from heart-easing words so long,
Begins to talk; but through his lips do throng
    Weak words so thick, come in his poor heart's aid,
    That no man could distinguish what he said.

Yet sometime, "Tarquin," was pronounced plain,
But through his teeth, as if the name he tore.
This windy tempest, till it blow up rain,
Held back his sorrow's tide, to make it more;
At last it rains, and busy winds give o'er:
    Then son and father weep with equal strife
    Who should weep most, for daughter or for wife.

The one doth call her his, the other his,
Yet neither may possess the claim they lay.
The father says, "She's mine." "O, mine she is!"
Replies her husband: "do not take away
My sorrow's interest; let no mourner say
    He weeps for her, for she was only mine,
    And only must be wail'd by Collatine."

"O," quoth Lucretius, "I did give that life
Which she too early and too late hath spill'd!"
"Woe, woe," quoth Collatine, "she was my wife,
I ow'd her, and 't is mine that she hath kill'd!"
"My daughter!" and "my wife!" with clamours fill'd

The dispers'd air, who, holding Lucrece' life,
Answer'd their cries, "my daughter!" and "my wife!"

Brutus, who pluck'd the knife from Lucrece' side,
Seeing such emulation in their woe,
Began to clothe his wit in state and pride,
Burying in Lucrece' wound his folly's show.
He with the Romans was esteemed so
    As silly-jeering idiots are with kings,
      For sportive words and uttering foolish things.

But now he throws that shallow habit by
Wherein deep policy did him disguise;
And arm'd his long-hid wits advisedly,
To check the tears in Collatinus' eyes.
"Thou wronged lord of Rome," quoth he, "arise;
    Let my unsounded self, suppos'd a fool,
      Now set thy long-experienc'd wit to school.

"Why, Collatine, is woe the cure for woe?
Do wounds help wounds, or grief help grievous deeds?
Is it revenge to give thyself a blow
For his foul act by whom thy fair wife bleeds?
Such childish humour from weak minds proceeds:
    Thy wretched wife mistook the matter so,
      To slay herself, that should have slain her foe.

"Courageous Roman, do not steep thy heart
In such relenting dew of lamentations,
But kneel with me, and help to bear thy part,
To rouse our Roman gods with invocations,
That they will suffer these abominations,
    Since Rome herself in them doth stand disgrac'd,
      By our strong arms from forth her fair streets chas'd.

"Now, by the Capitol that we adore,
And by this chaste blood so unjustly stain'd,
By heaven's fair sun that breeds the fat earth's store,
By all our country rights in Rome maintain'd,
And by her chaste Lucrece' soul that late complain'd
    Her wrongs to us, and by this bloody knife,
    We will revenge the death of this true wife!"

This said, he struck his hand upon his breast,
And kiss'd the fatal knife to end his vow;
And to his protestation urg'd the rest,
Who, wondering at him, did his words allow:
Then jointly to the ground their knees they bow;
    And that deep vow, which Brutus made before,
    He doth again repeat, and that they swore.

When they had sworn to this advised doom,
They did conclude to bear dead Lucrece thence;
To show her bleeding body thorough Rome,
And so to publish Tarquin's foul offence:
Which being done with speedy diligence,
    The Romans plausibly did give consent
    To Tarquin's everlasting banishment.

FINIS

A Lover's Complaint

A LOVER'S COMPLAINT

FROM off a hill whose concave womb re-worded
A plaintful story from a sistering vale,
My spirits to attend this double voice accorded,
And down I laid to list the sad-tun'd tale:
Ere long espied a fickle maid full pale,
Tearing of papers, breaking rings a-twain,
Storming her world with sorrow's wind and rain.

Upon her head a platted hive of straw,
Which fortified her visage from the sun,
Whereon the thought might think sometime it saw
The carcass of a beauty spent and done:
Time had not scythed all that youth begun,
Nor youth all quit; but, spite of heaven's fell rage,
Some beauty peep'd through lattice of sear'd age.

Oft did she heave her napkin to her eyne,
Which on it had conceited characters,

Laund'ring the silken figures in the brine
That season'd woe had pelleted in tears,
And often reading what contents it bears;
As often shrieking undistinguish'd woe,
In clamours of all size', both high and low.

Sometimes her levell'd eyes their carriage ride,
As they did battery to the spheres intend;
Sometime diverted their poor balls are tied
To th' orbed earth; sometimes they do extend
Their view right on; anon their gazes lend
To every place at once, and, nowhere fix'd,
The mind and sight distractedly commix'd.

Her hair, nor loose nor tied in formal plat,
Proclaim'd in her a careless hand of pride;
For some, untuck'd, descended her sheav'd hat,
Hanging her pale and pined cheek beside;
Some in her threaden fillet still did bide,
And, true to bondage, would not break from thence,
Though slackly braided in loose negligence.

A thousand favours from a maund she drew
Of amber, crystal, and of beaded jet,
Which one by one she in a river threw,
Upon whose weeping margent she was set;
Like usury, applying wet to wet,
Or monarch's hands, that let not bounty fall
Where want cries some, but where excess begs all.

Of folded schedules had she many a one,
Which she perus'd, sigh'd, tore, and gave the flood;
Crack'd many a ring of posied gold and bone,
Bidding them find their sepulchres in mud;
Found yet more letters sadly penn'd in blood,

With sleided silk feat and affectedly
Enswath'd, and seal'd to curious secrecy.

These often bath'd she in her fluxive eyes,
And often kiss'd, and often gan to tear;
Cried, "O false blood, thou register of lies,
What unapproved witness dost thou bear!
Ink would have seem'd more black and damned here!"
This said, in top of rage the lines she rents,
Big discontent so breaking their contents.

A reverend man that graz'd his cattle nigh,—
Sometime a blusterer, that the ruffle knew
Of court, of city, and had let go by
The swiftest hours, observed as they flew,—
Towards this afflicted fancy fastly drew;
And, privileg'd by age, desires to know
In brief the grounds and motives of her woe.

So slides he down upon his grained bat,
And comely-distant sits he by her side;
When he again desires her, being sat,
Her grievance with his hearing to divide:
If that from him there may be aught applied
Which may her suffering ecstasy assuage,
'Tis promis'd in the charity of age.

"Father," she says, "though in me you behold
The injury of many a blasting hour,
Let it not tell your judgment I am old;
Not age, but sorrow, over me hath power:
I might as yet have been a spreading flower,
Fresh to myself, if I had self-applied
Love to myself, and to no love beside.

"But, woe is me! too early I attended
A youthful suit (it was to gain my grace)
Of one by nature's outwards so commended,
That maidens' eyes stuck over all his face:
Love lack'd a dwelling, and made him her place;
And when in his fair parts she did abide,
She was new lodg'd, and newly deified.

"His browny locks did hang in crooked curls;
And every light occasion of the wind
Upon his lips their silken parcels hurls.
What's sweet to do, to do will aptly find:
Each eye that saw him did enchant the mind;
For on his visage was in little drawn,
What largeness thinks in paradise was sawn.

"Small show of man was yet upon his chin;
His phœnix down began but to appear,
Like unshorn velvet, on that termless skin,
Whose bare out-bragg'd the web it seem'd to wear;
Yet show'd his visage by that cost more dear;
And nice affections wavering stood in doubt
If best were as it was, or best without.

"His qualities were beauteous as his form,
For maiden-tongu'd he was, and thereof free;
Yet, if men mov'd him, was he such a storm
As oft 'twixt May and April is to see,
When winds breathe sweet, unruly though they be.
His rudeness so with his authóriz'd youth
Did livery falseness in a pride of truth.

"Well could he ride, and often men would say
'That horse his mettle from his rider takes:

Proud of subjection, noble by the sway,
What rounds, what bounds, what course, what stop he makes!'
And controversy hence a question takes,
Whether the horse by him became his deed,
Or he his manage by the well-doing steed.

"But quickly on this side the verdict went;
His real habitude gave life and grace
To appertainings and to ornament,
Accomplish'd in himself, not in his case:
All aids, themselves made fairer by their place,
Came for additions; yet their purpos'd trim
Piec'd not his grace, but were all grac'd by him.

"So on the tip of his subduing tongue
All kind of arguments and question deep.
All replication prompt, and reason strong,
For his advantage still did wake and sleep:
To make the weeper laugh, the laugher weep,
He had the dialect and different skill,
Catching all passions in his craft of will:

"That he did in the general bosom reign
Of young, of old; and sexes both enchanted
To dwell with him in thoughts, or to remain
In personal duty, following where he haunted:
Consents bewitch'd, ere he desire, have granted;
And dialogu'd for him what he would say,
Ask'd their own wills, and made their wills obey.

"Many there were that did his picture get,
To serve their eyes, and in it put their mind;
Like fools that in th' imagination set
The goodly objects which abroad they find
Of lands and mansions, theirs in thought assign'd;

And labouring in more pleasures to bestow them
Than the true gouty landlord which doth owe them:

"So many have, that never touch'd his hand,
Sweetly suppos'd them mistress of his heart.
My woeful self, that did in freedom stand,
And was my own fee-simple, (not in part)
What with his art in youth, and youth in art,
Threw my affections in his charmed power,
Reserv'd the stalk, and gave him all my flower.

"Yet did I not, as some my equals did,
Demand of him, nor being desir'd yielded;
Finding myself in honour so forbid,
With safest distance I mine honour shielded:
Experience for me many bulwarks builded
Of proofs new-bleeding, which remain'd the foil
Of this false jewel, and his amorous spoil.

"But, ah, who ever shunn'd by precedent
The destin'd ill she must herself assay?
Or forc'd examples, 'gainst her own content,
To put the by-pass'd perils in her way?
Counsel may stop a while what will not stay;
For when we rage, advice is often seen
By blunting us to make our wits more keen.

"Nor gives it satisfaction to our blood,
That we must curb it upon others' proof;
To be forbid the sweets that seem so good,
For fear of harms that preach in our behoof.
O appetite, from judgment stand aloof!
The one a palate hath that needs will taste,
Though Reason weep, and cry, 'It is thy last.'

"For further I could say, 'This man's untrue,'
And knew the patterns of his foul beguiling;
Heard where his plants in others' orchards grew,
Saw how deceits were gilded in his smiling;
Knew vows were ever brokers to defiling;
Thought characters and words merely but art,
And bastards of his foul adulterate heart.

"And long upon these terms I held my city,
Till thus he 'gan besiege me: 'Gentle maid,
Have of my suffering youth some feeling pity,
And be not of my holy vows afraid:
That's to you sworn, to none was ever said;
For feasts of love I have been called unto,
Till now did ne'er invite, nor never vow.

"'All my offences that abroad you see
Are errors of the blood, none of the mind;
Love made them not; with acture they may be,
Where neither party is nor true nor kind:
They sought their shame that so their shame did find;
And by so much less of shame in me remains,
By how much of me their reproach contains.

"'Among the many that mine eyes have seen,
Not one whose flame my heart so much as warm'd,
Or my affection put to the smallest teen,
Or any of my leisures ever charm'd:
Harm have I done to them, but ne'er was harm'd;
Kept hearts in liveries, but mine own was free,
And reign'd, commanding in his monarchy.

"'Look here what tributes wounded fancies sent me,
Of paled pearls, and rubies red as blood;

Figuring that they their passions likewise lent me
Of grief and blushes, aptly understood
In bloodless white and the encrimson'd mood;
Effects of terror and dear modesty,
Encamp'd in hearts, but fighting outwardly.

"'And, lo, behold these talents of their hair,
With twisted metal amorously impleach'd,
I have receiv'd from many a several fair,—
Their kind acceptance weepingly beseech'd,
With the annexions of fair gems enrich'd,
And deep-brain'd sonnets that did amplify
Each stone's dear nature, worth, and quality.

"'The diamond,—why, 'twas beautiful and hard,
Whereto his invis'd properties did tend;
The deep-green emerald, in whose fresh regard
Weak sights their sickly radiance do amend;
The heaven-hu'd sapphire and the opal blend
With objects manifold; each several stone,
With wit well blazon'd, smil'd or made some moan.

"'Lo, all these trophies of affections hot,
Of pensiv'd and subdu'd desires the tender,
Nature hath charg'd me that I hoard them not,
But yield them up where I myself must render,
That is, to you, my origin and ender;
For these, of force, must your oblations be,
Since I their altar, you enpatron me.

"'O, then, advance of yours that phraseless hand,
Whose white weighs down the airy scales of praise;
Take all these similes to your own command,
Hallow'd with sighs that burning lungs did raise;
What me your minister, for you obeys,

Works under you; and to your audit comes
Their distract parcels in combined sums.

"'Lo, this device was sent me from a nun,
Or sister sanctified, of holiest note;
Which late her noble suit in court did shun,
Whose rarest havings made the blossoms dote;
For she was sought by spirits of richest coat,
But kept cold distance, and did thence remove,
To spend her living in eternal love.

"'But, O, my sweet, what labour is't to leave
The thing we have not, mastering what not strives,—
Paling the place which did no form receive,
Playing patient sports in unconstrained gyves?
She that her fame so to herself contrives,
The scars of battle 'scapeth by the flight,
And makes her absence valiant, not her might.

"'O, pardon me, in that my boast is true;
The accident which brought me to her eye,
Upon the moment did her force subdue,
And now she would the caged cloister fly:
Religious love put out Religion's eye:
Not to be tempted, would she be immur'd,
And now, to tempt all, liberty procur'd.

"'How mighty then you are, O, hear me tell!
The broken bosoms that to me belong
Have emptied their fountains in my well,
And mine I pour your ocean all among:
I strong o'er them, and you o'er me being strong,
Must for your victory us all congest,
As compound love to physic your cold breast.

"'My parts had power to charm a sacred nun,
Who, disciplin'd, ay, dieted in grace,
Believ'd her eyes when they to assail begun,
All vows and consecrations giving place.
O, most potential love! vow, bond, nor space,
In thee hath neither sting, knot, nor confine,
For thou art all, and all things else are thine.

"'When thou impressest, what are precepts worth
Of stale example? When thou wilt inflame,
How coldly these impediments stand forth
Of wealth, of filial fear, law, kindred, fame!
Love's arms are peace, 'gainst rule, 'gainst sense, 'gainst shame,
And sweetens, in the suffering pangs it bears,
The aloes of all forces, shocks, and fears.

"'Now all these hearts that do on mine depend,
Feeling it break, with bleeding groans they pine,
And supplicant their sighs to you extend,
To leave the battery that you make 'gainst mine,
Lending soft audience to my sweet design,
And credent soul to that strong-bonded oath,
That shall prefer and undertake my troth.'

"This said, his watery eyes he did dismount
Whose sighs till then were levell'd on my face;
Each cheek a river running from a fount
With brinish current downward flow'd apace:
O, how the channel to the stream gave grace!
Who glaz'd with crystal gate the glowing roses
That flame through water which their hue encloses.

"O, father, what a hell of witchcraft lies
In the small orb of one particular tear!

But with the inundation of the eyes
What rocky heart to water will not wear?
What breast so cold that it is not warmed here?
O cleft effect! cold modesty, hot wrath,
Both fire from hence and chill extincture hath!

"For, lo, his passion, but an art of craft,
Even there resolv'd my reason into tears;
There my white stole of chastity I daff'd,
Shook off my sober guards and civil fears;
Appear to him, as he to me appears,
All melting, though our drops this difference bore,
His poison'd me, and mine did him restore.

"In him a plenitude of subtle matter,
Applied to cautels, all strange forms receives,
Of burning blushes, of weeping water,
Or swooning paleness; and he takes and leaves,
In either's aptness, as it best deceives,
To blush at speeches rank, to weep at woes,
Or to turn white and swoon at tragic shows;

"That not a heart which in his level came
Could scape the hail of his all-hurting aim,
Showing fair nature is both kind and tame;
And, veil'd in them, did win whom he would maim:
Against the thing he sought he would exclaim;
When he most burn'd in heart-wish'd luxury,
He preach'd pure maid, and prais'd cold chastity.

"Thus merely with the garment of a Grace
The naked and concealed fiend he cover'd,
That th' unexperient gave the tempter place,
Which, like a cherubin, above them hover'd.
Who, young and simple, would not be so lover'd?

Ah me! I fell; and yet do question make
What I should do again for such a sake.

"O, that infected moisture of his eye,
O, that false fire which in his cheek so glow'd,
O, that forc'd thunder from his heart did fly,
O, that sad breath his spongy lungs bestow'd,
O, all that borrow'd motion, seeming ow'd,
Would yet again betray the fore-betray'd,
And new pervert a reconciled maid!"

The Passionate Pilgrim

THE PASSIONATE PILGRIM

I

DID not the heavenly rhetoric of thine eye,
'Gainst whom the world could not hold argument,
Persuade my heart to his false perjury?
Vows for thee broke deserve not punishment.
A woman I foreswore; but, I will prove,
Thou being a goddess, I forswore not thee:
My vow was earthly, thou a heavenly love;
Thy grave being gain'd cures all disgrace in me.
My vow was breath, and breath a vapour is;
Then, thou fair sun, that on this earth doth shine,
Exhale this vapour vow; in thee it is:
If broken then, it is no fault of mine.
    If by me broke, what fool is not so wise
    To lose an oath to win a paradise?

II

Sweet Cytherea, sitting by a brook,
With young Adonis, lovely-fresh and green,
Did court the lad with many a lovely look,—
Such looks as none could look but beauty's queen.
She told him stories to delight his ear;
She show'd him favours to allure his eye;
To win his heart, she touch'd him here and there,—
Touches so soft still conquer chastity,—
But whether unripe years did want conceit,
Or he refus'd to take her figur'd proffer,
The tender nibbler would not touch the bait,
But smile and jest at every gentle offer:
    Then fell she on her back, fair queen and toward;
    He ran and ran away,—ah, fool too froward!

III

If love make me forsworn, how shall I swear to love?
O, never faith could hold, if not to beauty vow'd!
Though to myself forsworn, to thee I'll constant prove;
Those thoughts to me like oaks, to thee like osiers bow'd.
Study his bias leaves, and makes his book thine eyes,
Where all those pleasures live that art can comprehend.
If knowledge be the mark, to know thee shall suffice;
Well learned is that tongue that well can thee commend;
All ignorant that soul that sees thee without wonder;
Which is to me some praise, that I thy parts admire:
Thine eye Jove's lightning seems, thy voice his dreadful thunder,
Which, not to anger bent, is music and sweet fire.
    Celestial as thou art, O, do not love that wrong,
    To sing the heavens' praise with such an earthly tongue!

IV

Scarce had the sun dried up the dewy morn,
And scarce the herd gone to the hedge for shade,
When Cytherea, all in love forlorn,
A longing tarriance for Adonis made
Under an osier growing by a brook,
A brook where Adon used to cool his spleen:
Hot was the day; she hotter than did look
For his approach, that often there had been.
Anon he comes, and throws his mantle by,
And stood stark naked on the brook's green brim:
The sun look'd on the world with glorious eye,
Yet not so wistly as this queen on him:
    He, spying her, bounc'd in, whereas he stood;
    "O Jove," quoth she, "why was not I a flood!"

V

Fair is my love, but not so fair as fickle;
Mild as a dove, but neither true nor trusty;
Brighter than glass, and yet, as glass is, brittle;
Softer than wax, and yet, as iron, rusty:
    A lily pale, with damask dye to grace her,
    None fairer, nor none falser to deface her.

Her lips to mine how often hath she join'd,
Between each kiss her oaths of true love swearing!
How many tales to please me hath she coin'd,
Dreading my love, the loss thereof still fearing!
    Yet in the midst of all her pure protestings,
    Her faith, her oaths, her tears, and all were jestings.

She burn'd with love, as straw with fire flameth,
She burn'd out love, as soon as straw out-burneth;
She fram'd the love, and yet she foil'd the framing,
She bade love last, and yet she fell a-turning.
    Was this a lover, or a lecher whether?
    Bad in the best, though excellent in neither.

VI

If music and sweet poetry agree,
As they must needs, the sister and the brother,
Then must the love be great 'twixt thee and me,
Because thou lov'st the one, and I the other.
Dowland to thee is dear, whose heavenly touch
Upon the lute doth ravish human sense;
Spenser to me, whose deep conceit is such,
As, passing all conceit, needs no defence.
Thou lov'st to hear the sweet melodious sound
That Phœbus' lute, the queen of music, makes;
And I in deep delight am chiefly drown'd,
Whenas himself to singing he betakes.
    One god is god of both, as poets feign;
    One knight loves both, and both in thee remain.

VII

Fair was the morn, when the fair queen of love,
  *   *   *   *   *   *   *   *[a]
Paler for sorrow than her milk-white dove,
For Adon's sake, a youngster proud and wild;
Her stand she takes upon a steep-up hill:
Anon Adonis comes with horn and hounds;
She, silly queen, with more than love's good will,
Forbade the boy he should not pass those grounds;

[a] A line was lost here.

"Once," quoth she, "did I see a fair sweet youth
Here in these brakes deep-wounded with a boar,
Deep in the thigh, a spectacle of ruth!
See in my thigh," quoth she, "here was the sore":
　　She showed hers; he saw more wounds than one,
　　And blushing fled, and left her all alone.

VIII

Sweet rose, fair flower, untimely pluck'd, soon faded,
Pluck'd in the bud, and faded in the spring!
Bright orient pearl, alack! too timely shaded!
Fair creature, kill'd too soon by death's sharp sting!
　　Like a green plum that hangs upon a tree,
　　And falls, through wind, before the fall should be.

I weep for thee, and yet no cause I have;
For why thou left'st me nothing in thy will:
And yet thou left'st me more than I did crave;
For why I craved nothing of thee still:
　　O yes, dear friend, I pardon crave of thee,—
　　Thy discontent thou didst bequeath to me.

IX

Venus, with young Adonis sitting by her
Under a myrtle shade, began to woo him:
She told the youngling how god Mars did try her,
And as he fell to her, so fell she to him.
"Even thus," quoth she, "the warlike god embrac'd me,"
And then she clipp'd Adonis in her arms;
"Even thus," quoth she, "the warlike god unlac'd me,"
As if the boy should use like loving charms;

"Even thus," quoth she, "he seized on my lips,"
And with her lips on his did act the seizure;
And as she fetched breath, away he skips,
And would not take her meaning nor her pleasure.
    Ah, that I had that lady at this bay,
    To kiss and clip me till I run away!

X

Crabbed age and youth
    Cannot live together:
Youth is full of pleasance,
    Age is full of care;
Youth like summer morn,
    Age like winter weather;
Youth like summer brave,
    Age like winter bare.
Youth is full of sport,
Age's breath is short;
    Youth is nimble, age is lame;
Youth is hot and bold,
Age is weak and cold;
    Youth is wild, and age is tame.
Age, I do abhor thee,
Youth, I do adore thee;
    O, my love, my love is young!
Age, I do defy thee:—
O, sweet shepherd, hie thee!
    For methinks thou stay'st too long.

XI

Beauty is but a vain and doubtful good,
A shining gloss that fadeth suddenly;
A flower that dies when first it 'gins to bud;
A brittle glass that's broken presently:
    A doubtful good, a gloss, a glass, a flower,
    Lost, faded, broken, dead within an hour!

And as goods lost are seld or never found,
As faded gloss no rubbing will refresh,
As flowers dead lie wither'd on the ground,
As broken glass no cement can redress,—
    So beauty blemish'd once for ever's lost,
    In spite of physic, painting, pain, and cost.

XII

"Good night, good rest." Ah, neither be my share!
She bade good night, that kept my rest away;
And daff'd me to a cabin hang'd with care,
To descant on the doubts of my decay.
    "Farewell," quoth she, "and come again tomorrow";
    Fare well I could not, for I supp'd with sorrow.

Yet at my parting sweetly did she smile,
In scorn or friendship, nill I construe whether:
'T may be, she joy'd to jest at my exile,
'T may be, again to make me wander thither:
    "Wander!" a word for shadows like myself,
    As take the pain, but cannot pluck the pelf.

XIII

Lord, how mine eyes throw gazes to the east!
My heart doth charge the watch; the morning rise
Doth cite each moving sense from idle rest.
Not daring trust the office of mine eyes,
    While Philomela sits and sings, I sit and mark,
    And wish her lays were tuned like the lark;

For she doth welcome daylight with her ditty,
And drives away dark dismal-dreaming night:
The night so pack'd, I post unto my pretty;
Heart hath his hope, and eyes their wished sight;
    Sorrow chang'd to solace, solace mix'd with sorrow;
    For why she sigh'd, and bade me come tomorrow.

Were I with her, the night would post too soon;
But now are minutes added to the hours;
To spite me now, each minute seems a moon;
Yet not for me, shine sun to succour flowers!
    Pack night, peep day; good day, of night now borrow;
    Short, night, to-night, and length thyself tomorrow.

Sonnets to Sundry Notes of Music

SONNETS TO SUNDRY
NOTES OF MUSIC

I

It was a lording's daughter,
The fairest one of three,
That liked of her master
As well as well might be,
Till looking on an Englishman,
The fair'st that eye could see,
    Her fancy fell a-turning.

Long was the combat doubtful
That love with love did fight,
To leave the master loveless,
Or kill the gallant knight:
To put in practice either,
Alas, it was a spite
    Unto the silly damsel!

But one must be refused;
More mickle was the pain,
That nothing could be used
To turn them both to gain,
For of the two the trusty knight
Was wounded with disdain:
    Alas, she could not help it!

Thus art, with arms contending,
Was victor of the day,
Which by a gift of learning
Did bear the maid away:
Then, lullaby, the learned man
Hath got the lady gay;
    For now my song is ended.

II

On a day (alack the day!),
Love, whose month was ever May,
Spy'd a blossom passing fair,
Playing in the wanton air:
Through the velvet leaves the wind,
All unseen, 'gan passage find;
That the lover, sick to death,
Wish'd himself the heaven's breath.

"Air," quoth he, "thy cheeks may blow;
Air, would I might triumph so!
But, alas, my hand hath sworn
Ne'er to pluck thee from thy thorn!
Vow, alack, for youth unmeet,
Youth so apt to pluck a sweet.
Thou for whom Jove would swear
Juno but an Ethiope were;
And deny himself for Jove,
Turning mortal for thy love."

III

My flocks feed not,
My ewes breed not,
My rams speed not,
 All is amiss:
Love's denying,
Faith's defying,
Heart's renying,
 Causer of this.
All my merry jigs are quite forgot,
All my lady's love is lost, God wot:
Where her faith was firmly fix'd in love,
There a nay is plac'd without remove.
One silly cross
Wrought all my loss;
 O, frowning Fortune, cursed, fickle dame!
For now I see,
Inconstancy
 More in women than in men remain.

In black mourn I,
All fears scorn I,
Love hath forlorn me,
    Living in thrall:
Heart is bleeding,
All help needing,—
O cruel speeding!—
    Fraughted with gall!
My shepherd's pipe can sound no deal,
My wether's bell rings doleful knell;
My curtail dog, that wont to have play'd,
Plays not at all, but seems afraid;
My sighs so deep,
Procure to weep,
    In howling wise, to see my doleful plight.
How sighs resound
Through heartless ground,
    Like a thousand vanquish'd men in bloody fight!

Clear wells spring not,
Sweet birds sing not,
Green plants bring not
    Forth their dye:
Herds stand weeping,
Flocks all sleeping,
Nymphs back peeping
    Fearfully:
All our pleasure known to us poor swains,
All our merry meetings on the plains,
All our evening sport from us is fled,
All our love is lost, for Love is dead.
Farewell, sweet lass,
Thy like ne'er was
    For a sweet content, the cause of all my moan:
Poor Coridon

Must live alone,
    Other help for him I see that there is none.

IV

Whenas thine eye hath chose the dame,
And stall'd the deer that thou shouldst strike,
Let reason rule things worthy blame,
As well as fancy partial might:
    Take counsel of some wiser head,
    Neither too young, nor yet unwed.

And when thou com'st thy tale to tell,
Smooth not thy tongue with filed talk,
Lest she some subtle practice smell,—
A cripple soon can find a halt;—
    But plainly say thou lov'st her well,
    And set thy person forth to sell.

What though her frowning brows be bent,
Her cloudy looks will clear ere night;
And then too late she will repent,
That thus dissembled her delight;
    And twice desire, ere it be day,
    That which with scorn she put away.

What though she strive to try her strength,
And ban and brawl, and say thee nay,
Her feeble force will yield at length,
When craft hath taught her thus to say,—
    "Had women been so strong as men,
    In faith you had not had it then."

And to her will frame all thy ways;
Spare not to spend,—and chiefly there
Where thy desert may merit praise,
By ringing in thy lady's ear:
    The strongest castle, tower, and town,
    The golden bullet beats it down.

Serve always with assured trust,
And in thy suit be humble-true;
Unless thy lady prove unjust,
Seek never thou to choose anew:
    When time shall serve, be thou not slack
    To proffer, though she put thee back.

The wiles and guiles that women work,
Dissembled with an outward show,
The tricks and toys that in them lurk,
The cock that treads them shall not know.
    Have you not heard it said full oft,
    A woman's nay doth stand for nought?

Think women love to match with men,
And not to live so like a saint:
Here is no heaven; they holy then
Begin when age does them attaint.
    Were kisses all the joys in bed,
    One woman would another wed.

But soft! enough,—too much I fear;
For if my mistress hear my song;
She will not stick to ring mine ear,
To teach my tongue to be so long;
    Yet will she blush, here be it said,
    To hear her secrets so bewray'd.

V

Live with me, and be my love,
And we will all the pleasures prove
That hills and valleys, dales and fields,
And all the craggy mountain yields.

There will we sit upon the rocks,
And see the shepherds feed their flocks,
By shallow rivers, to whose falls
Melodious birds sing madrigals.

There will I make thee a bed of roses,
With a thousand fragrant posies,
A cap of flowers, and a kirtle,
Embroider'd all with leaves of myrtle.

A belt of straw and ivy buds,
With coral clasps and amber studs;
And if these pleasures may thee move,
Then, live with me and be my love.

LOVE'S ANSWER

If that the world and love were young,
And truth in every shepherd's tongue,
These pretty pleasures might me move
To live with thee and be thy love.

VI

As it fell upon a day
In the merry month of May,

Sitting in a pleasant shade
Which a grove of myrtles made,
Beasts did leap, and birds did sing,
Trees did grow, and plants did spring;
Everything did banish moan,
Save the nightingale alone:
She, poor bird, as all forlorn,
Lean'd her breast up-till a thorn,
And there sung the dolefull'st ditty,
That to hear it was great pity:
"Fie, fie, fie," now would she cry,
"Tereu, tereu!" by and by;
That to hear her so complain,
Scarce I could from tears refrain;
For her griefs, so lively shown,
Made me think upon mine own.
Ah, thought I, thou mourn'st in vain!
None takes pity on thy pain:
Senseless trees they cannot hear thee;
Ruthless beasts they will not cheer thee,
King Pandion he is dead;
All thy friends are lapp'd in lead;
All thy fellow-birds do sing,
Careless of thy sorrowing.
Even so, poor bird, like thee,
None alive will pity me.

VII

Whilst as fickle Fortune smil'd,
Thou and I were both beguil'd:
Every one that flatters thee
Is no friend in misery.

Words are easy, like the wind;
Faithful friends are hard to find:
Every man will be thy friend,
Whilst thou hast wherewith to spend;
But if store of crowns be scant,
No man will supply thy want.
If that one be prodigal,
Bountiful they will him call:
And with such-like flattering,
Pity but he were a king.
If he be addict to vice,
Quickly him they will entice;
If to women he be bent,
They have him at commandement;
But if fortune once do frown,
Then farewell his great renown;
They that fawn'd on him before,
Use his company no more.
He that is thy friend indeed,
He will help thee in thy need;
If thou sorrow, he will weep;
If thou wake, he cannot sleep:
Thus of every grief in heart
He with thee doth bear a part.
These are certain signs to know
Faithful friend from flattering foe.

The Phoenix and Turtle

THE PHOENIX AND TURTLE

FROM THE ADDITIONAL
POEMS TO CHESTER'S

Love's Martyr, or Rosalin's Complaint, 1601

LET the bird of loudest lay,
On the sole Arabian tree,
Herald sad and trumpet be,
To whose sound chaste wings obey.

But thou shrieking harbinger,
Foul pre-currer of the fiend,
Augur of the fever's end,
To this troop come thou not near!

From this session interdict
Every foul of tyrant wing,
Save the eagle, feather'd king:
Keep the obsequy so strict.

Let the priest in surplice white,
That defunctive music can,
Be the death-divining swan,
Lest the requiem lack his right.

And thou, treble-dated crow,
That thy sable gender mak'st
With the breath thou giv'st and tak'st,
'Mongst our mourners shalt thou go.

Here the anthem doth commence:—
Love and constancy is dead;
Phoenix and the turtle fled
In a mutual flame from hence.

So they lov'd, as love in twain
Had the essence but in one;
Two distincts, division none:
Number there in love was slain.

Hearts remote, yet not asunder;
Distance, and no space was seen
'Twixt the turtle and his queen:
But in them it were a wonder.

So between them love did shine,
That the turtle saw his right
Flaming in the phoenix' sight;
Either was the other's mine.

Property was thus appall'd,
That the self was not the same
Single nature's double name
Neither two nor one was call'd.

Reason, in itself confounded,
Saw division grow together;
To themselves yet either-neither,
Simple were so well compounded;

That it cried, How true a twain
Seemeth this concordant one!
Love hath reason, reason none,
If what parts can so remain.

Whereupon it made this threne
To the phoenix and the dove,
Co-supremes and stars of love,
As chorus to their tragic scene.

THRENOS

Beauty, truth, and rarity,
Grace in all simplicity,
Here enclos'd in cinders lie.

· Death is now the phoenix' nest;
And the turtle's loyal breast
To eternity doth rest,

Leaving no posterity:—
'Twas not their infirmity,
It was married chastity.

Truth may seem, but cannot be;
Beauty, brag, but 't is not she;
Truth and beauty buried be.

To this urn let those repair
That are either true or fair;
For these dead birds sigh a prayer.

Sonnets

SONNETS

I

From fairest creatures we desire increase,
That thereby beauty's rose might never die,
But as the riper should by time decease,
His tender heir might bear his memory:
But thou, contracted to thine own bright eyes,
Feed'st thy light's flame with self-substantial fuel,
Making a famine where abundance lies,
Thyself thy foe, to thy sweet self too cruel.
Thou that art now the world's fresh ornament,
And only herald to the gaudy spring,
Within thine own bud buriest thy content,
And, tender churl, mak'st waste in niggarding.
    Pity the world, or else this glutton be,
      To eat the world's due, by the grave and thee.

II

When forty winters shall besiege thy brow,
And dig deep trenches in thy beauty's field,
Thy youth's proud livery, so gaz'd on now,
Will be a tatter'd weed, of small worth held:
Then being ask'd where all thy beauty lies,
Where all the treasure of thy lusty days,—
To say, within thine own deep-sunken eyes,
Were an all-eating shame and thriftless praise.
How much more praise deserv'd thy beauty's use,
If thou couldst answer—"This fair child of mine
Shall sum my count, and make my old excuse,—"
Proving his beauty by succession thine!
  This were to be new-made when thou art old,
  And see thy blood warm when thou feel'st it cold.

III

Look in thy glass, and tell the face thou viewest,
Now is the time that face should form another;
Whose fresh repair if now thou not renewest,
Thou dost beguile the world, unbless some mother.
For where is she so fair whose unear'd womb
Disdains the tillage of thy husbandry?
Or who is he so fond will be the tomb
Of his self-love, to stop posterity?
Thou art thy mother's glass, and she in thee
Calls back the lovely April of her prime:
So thou through windows of thine age shalt see,
Despite of wrinkles, this thy golden time.
  But if thou live, remember'd not to be,
  Die single, and thine image dies with thee.

IV

Unthrifty loveliness, why dost thou spend
Upon thyself thy beauty's legacy?
Nature's bequest gives nothing, but doth lend,
And, being frank, she lends to those are free.
Then, beauteous niggard, why dost thou abuse
The bounteous largess given thee to give?
Profitless usurer, why dost thou use
So great a sum of sums, yet canst not live?
For having traffic with thyself alone,
Thou of thyself thy sweet self dost deceive.
Then how, when nature calls thee to be gone,
What acceptable audit canst thou leave?
    Thy unus'd beauty must be tomb'd with thee,
    Which, used, lives th' executor to be.

V

Those hours, that with gentle work did frame
The lovely gaze where every eye doth dwell,
Will play the tyrants to the very same,
And that unfair which fairly doth excel;
For never-resting time leads summer on
To hideous winter, and confounds him there;
Sap check'd with frost, and lusty leaves quite gone,
Beauty o'ersnow'd, and bareness everywhere:
Then, were not summer's distillation left,
A liquid prisoner pent in walls of glass,
Beauty's effect with beauty were bereft,
Nor it, nor no remembrance what it was:
    But flowers distill'd, though they with winter meet,
    Leese but their show; their substance still lives sweet.

VI

Then let not winter's ragged hand deface
In thee thy summer, ere thou be distill'd:
Make sweet some phial; treasure thou some place
With beauty's treasure, ere it be self-kill'd.
That use is not forbidden usury,
Which happies those that pay the willing loan;
That's for thyself to breed another thee,
Or ten times happier, be it ten for one;
Ten times thyself were happier than thou art,
If ten of thine ten times refigur'd thee:
Then what could death do if thou shouldst depart,
Leaving thee living in posterity?
　　Be not self-will'd, for thou art much too fair
　　To be Death's conquest, and make worms thine heir.

VII

Lo, in the orient when the gracious light
Lifts up his burning head, each under eye
Doth homage to his new-appearing sight,
Serving with looks his sacred majesty;
And having climb'd the steep up heavenly hill,
Resembling strong youth in his middle age,
Yet mortal looks adore his beauty still,
Attending on his golden pilgrimage;
But when from high-most pitch, with weary car,
Like feeble age, he reeleth from the day,
The eyes, 'fore duteous, now converted are
From his low tract, and look another way:
　　So thou, thyself out-going in thy noon,
　　Unlook'd on diest, unless thou get a son.

VIII

Music to hear, why hear'st thou music sadly?
Sweets with sweets war not, joy delights in joy.
Why lov'st thou that which thou receiv'st not gladly,
Or else receiv'st with pleasure thine annoy?
If the true concord of well-tuned sounds,
By unions married, do offend thine ear,
They do but sweetly chide thee, who confounds
In singleness the parts that thou shouldst bear.
Mark how one string, sweet husband to another,
Strikes each in each by mutual ordering;
Resembling sire and child and happy mother,
Who, all in one, one pleasing note do sing:
    Whose speechless song, being many, seeming one,
    Sings this to thee, "thou single wilt prove none."

IX

Is it for fear to wet a widow's eye
That thou consum'st thyself in single life?
Ah! if thou issueless shalt hap to die,
The world will wail thee, like a makeless wife;
The world will be thy widow, and still weep
That thou no form of thee hast left behind,
When every private widow well may keep,
By children's eyes, her husband's shape in mind.
Look, what an unthrift in the world doth spend
Shifts but his place, for still the world enjoys it;
But beauty's waste hath in the world an end,
And kept unus'd, the user so destroys it.
    No love toward others in that bosom sits
    That on himself such murderous shame commits.

X

For shame, deny that thou bear'st love to any,
Who for thyself art so unprovident.
Grant, if thou wilt, thou art belov'd of many,
But that thou none lov'st is most evident;
For thou art so possess'd with murderous hate,
That 'gainst thyself thou stick'st not to conspire,
Seeking that beauteous roof to ruinate,
Which to repair should be thy chief desire.
O, change thy thought, that I may change my mind!
Shall hate be fairer lodg'd than gentle love?
Be, as thy presence is, gracious and kind,
Or to thyself, at least, kind-hearted prove:
    Make thee another self, for love of me,
    That beauty still may live in thine or thee.

XI

As fast as thou shalt wane, so fast thou growest
In one of thine, from that which thou departest;
And that fresh blood which youngly thou bestowest,
Thou mayst call thine, when thou from youth convertest.
Herein lives wisdom, beauty, and increase;
Without this, folly, age, and cold decay:
If all were minded so, the times should cease,
And threescore year would make the world away.
Let those whom Nature hath not made for store,
Harsh, featureless, and rude, barrenly perish:
Look, whom she best endow'd, she gave thee more,
Which bounteous gift thou shouldst in bounty cherish;
    She carv'd thee for her seal, and meant thereby
    Thou shouldst print more, nor let that copy die.

XII

When I do count the clock that tells the time,
And see the brave day sunk in hideous night;
When I behold the violet past prime,
And sable curls all silver'd o'er with white;
When lofty trees I see barren of leaves,
Which erst from heat did canopy the herd,
And summer's green, all girded up in sheaves,
Borne on the bier with white and bristly beard;
Then of thy beauty do I question make,
That thou among the wastes of time must go,
Since sweets and beauties do themselves forsake,
And die as fast as they see others grow;
    And nothing 'gainst Time's scythe can make defence
    Save breed, to brave him when he takes thee hence.

XIII

O, that you were yourself! but, love, you are
No longer yours than you yourself here live:
Against this coming end you should prepare,
And your sweet semblance to some other give.
So should that beauty which you hold in lease
Find no determination; then you were
Yourself again, after yourself's decease,
When your sweet issue your sweet form should bear.
Who lets so fair a house fall to decay,
Which husbandry in honour might uphold
Against the stormy gusts of winter's day,
And barren rage of death's eternal cold?
    O, none but unthrifts!—dear my love, you know
    You had a father; let your son say so.

XIV

Not from the stars do I my judgment pluck;
And yet methinks I have astronomy,
But not to tell of good or evil luck,
Of plagues, of dearths, or seasons' quality:
Nor can I fortune to brief minutes tell,
'Pointing to each his thunder, rain, and wind,
Or say with princes if it shall go well,
By oft predict that I in heaven find:
But from thine eyes my knowledge I derive,
And, constant stars, in them I read such art,
As truth and beauty shall together thrive.
If from thyself to store thou wouldst convert;
 Or else of thee this I prognosticate,—
 Thy end is truth's and beauty's doom and date.

XV

When I consider everything that grows
Holds in perfection but a little moment,
That this huge stage presenteth nought but shows
Whereon the stars in secret influence comment;
When I perceive that men as plants decrease,
Cheered and check'd even by the self-same sky;
Vaunt in their youthful sap, at height decrease,
And wear their brave state out of memory;
Then the conceit of this inconstant stay
Sets you most rich in youth before my sight,
Where wasteful Time debateth with Decay,
To change your day of youth to sullied night;
 And, all in war with Time, for love of you,
 As he takes from you, I engraft you new.

XVI

But wherefore do not you a mightier way
Make war upon this bloody tyrant, Time?
And fortify yourself in your decay
With means more blessed than my barren rhyme?
Now stand you on the top of happy hours;
And many maiden gardens, yet unset,
With virtuous wish would bear your living flowers,
Much liker than your painted counterfeit:
So should the lines of life that life repair,
Which this, Time's pencil, or my pupil pen,
Neither in inward worth nor outward fair,
Can make you live yourself in eyes of men.
>   To give away yourself keeps yourself still;
>   And you must live, drawn by your own sweet skill.

XVII

Who will believe my verse in time to come,
If it were fill'd with your most high deserts?
Though yet, heaven knows, it is but as a tomb
Which hides your life, and shows not half your parts.
If I could write the beauty of your eyes,
And in fresh numbers number all your graces,
The age to come would say, "This poet lies,
Such heavenly touches ne'er touch'd earthly faces."
So should my papers, yellow'd with their age,
Be scorn'd, like old men of less truth than tongue;
And your true rights be term'd a poet's rage,
And stretched metre of an antique song:
>   But were some child of yours alive that time,
>   You should live twice;—in it, and in my rhyme.

XVIII

Shall I compare thee to a summer's day?
Thou art more lovely and more temperate:
Rough winds do shake the darling buds of May,
And summer's lease hath all too short a date:
Sometime too hot the eye of heaven shines,
And often is his gold complexion dimm'd;
And every fair from fair sometime declines,
By chance, or nature's changing course, untrimm'd;
But thy eternal summer shall not fade,
Nor lose possession of that fair thou owest;
Nor shall Death brag thou wander'st in his shade,
When in eternal lines to time thou growest:
    So long as men can breathe, or eyes can see,
    So long lives this, and this gives life to thee.

XIX

Devouring Time, blunt thou the lion's paws,
And make the earth devour her own sweet brood;
Pluck the keen teeth from the fierce's tiger's jaws,
And burn the long-liv'd phoenix in her blood;
Make glad and sorry seasons as thou fleets,
And do whate'er thou wilt, swift-footed Time,
To the wide world and all her fading sweets;
But I forbid thee one most heinous crime:
O, carve not with thy hours my love's fair brow,
Nor draw no lines there with thine antique pen;
Him in thy course untainted do allow,
For beauty's pattern to succeeding men.
    Yet, do thy worst, old Time: despite thy wrong,
    My love shall in my verse ever live young.

XX

A woman's face, with Nature's own hand painted,
Hast thou, the master-mistress of my passion;
A woman's gentle heart, but not acquainted
With shifting change, as is false women's fashion;
An eye more bright than theirs, less false in rolling,
Gilding the object whereupon it gazeth;
A man in hue, all hues in his controlling,
Which steals men's eyes, and women's souls amazeth.
And for a woman wert thou first created;
Till Nature, as she wrought thee, fell a-doting,
And, by addition, me of thee defeated,
By adding one thing to my purpose nothing.
    But since she prick'd thee out for women's pleasure,
    Mine be thy love, and thy love's use their treasure.

XXI

So is it not with me as with that Muse,
Stirr'd by a painted beauty to his verse;
Who heaven itself for ornament doth use,
And every fair with his fair doth rehearse;
Making a couplement of proud compare,
With sun and moon, with earth and sea's rich gems,
With April's first-born flowers, and all things rare
That heaven's air in this huge rondure hems.
O, let me, true in love, but truly write,
And then believe me, my love is as fair
As any mother's child, though not so bright
As those gold candles fix'd in heaven's air:
    Let them say more that like of hearsay well;
    I will not praise that purpose not to sell.

XXII

My glass shall not persuade me I am old,
So long as youth and thou are of one date;
But when in thee time's furrows I behold,
Then look I death my days should expiate.
For all that beauty that doth cover thee
Is but the seemly raiment of my heart,
Which in thy breast doth live, as thine in me:
How can I, then, be elder than thou art?
O, therefore, love, be of thyself so wary,
As I, not for myself, but for thee will;
Bearing thy heart, which I will keep so chary
As tender nurse her babe from faring ill.
    Presume not on thy heart when mine is slain;
    Thou gav'st me thine, not to give back again.

XXIII

As an unperfect actor on the stage,
Who with his fear is put besides his part,
Or some fierce thing replete with too much rage,
Whose strength's abundance weakens his own heart;
So I, for fear of trust, forget to say
The perfect ceremony of love's rite,
And in mine own love's strength seem to decay,
O'ercharg'd with burden of mine own love's might.
O, let my books be, then, the eloquence
And dumb presagers of my speaking breast;
Who plead for love, and look for recompence,
More than that tongue that more hath more express'd.
    O, learn to read what silent love hath writ:
    To hear with eyes belongs to love's fine wit.

XXIV

Mine eye hath play'd the painter, and hath stell'd
Thy beauty's form in table of my heart;
My body is the frame wherein 'tis held,
And pérspective it is best painter's art.
For through the painter must you see his skill,
To find where your true image pictur'd lies,
Which in my bosom's shop is hanging still,
That hath his windows glazed with thine eyes.
Now see what good turns eyes for eyes have done;
Mine eyes have drawn thy shape, and thine for me
Are windows to my breast, where-through the sun
Delights to peep, to gaze therein on thee;
    Yet eyes this cunning want to grace their art,
    They draw but what they see, know not the heart.

XXV

Let those who are in favour with their stars,
Of public honour and proud titles boast,
Whilst I, whom fortune of such triumph bars,
Unlook'd for joy in that I honour most.
Great princes' favourites their fair leaves spread
But as the marigold at the sun's eye;
And in themselves their pride lies buried,
For at a frown they in their glory die.
The painful warrior famoused for fight,
After a thousand victories once foil'd,
Is from the book of honour razed quite,
And all the rest forgot for which he toil'd:
    Then happy I, that love and am belov'd
    Where I may not remove nor be remov'd.

XXVI

Lord of my love, to whom in vassalage
Thy merit hath my duty strongly knit,
To thee I send this written embassage,
To witness duty, not to show my wit;
Duty so great, which wit so poor as mine
May make seem bare, in wanting words to show it;
But that I hope some good conceit of thine
In thy soul's thought, all naked, will bestow it;
Till whatsoever star that guides by moving,
Points on me graciously with fair aspéct,
And puts apparel on my tatter'd loving,
To show me worthy of thy sweet respect:
    Then may I dare to boast how I do love thee;
    Till then not show my head where thou mayst prove me.

XXVII

Weary with toil, I haste me to my bed,
The dear repose for limbs with travel tir'd;
But then begins a journey in my head,
To work my mind, when body's work 's expir'd:
For then my thoughts (from far where I abide)
Intend a zealous pilgrimage to thee,
And keep my drooping eyelids open wide,
Looking on darkness which the blind do see:
Save that my soul's imaginary sight
Presents thy shadow to my sightless view,
Which, like a jewel hung in ghastly night,
Makes black night beauteous, and her old face new.
    Lo, thus, by day my limbs, by night my mind,
    For thee and for myself no quiet find.

XXVIII

How can I, then, return in happy plight,
That am debarr'd the benefit of rest?
When day's oppression is not eas'd by night,
But day by night, and night by day, oppress'd?
And each, though enemies to either's reign,
Do in consent shake hands to torture me;
The one by toil, the other to complain
How far I toil, still farther off from thee.
I tell the day, to please him, thou art bright,
And dost him grace when clouds do blot the heaven:
So flatter I the swart-complexion'd night,
When sparkling stars twire not, thou gild'st the even.
    But day doth daily draw my sorrows longer,
    And night doth nightly make grief's strength seem stronger.

XXIX

When in disgrace with fortune and men's eyes,
I all alone beweep my outcast state,
And trouble deaf heaven with my bootless cries,
And look upon myself, and curse my fate,
Wishing me like to one more rich in hope,
Featur'd like him, like him with friends possess'd,
Desiring this man's art, and that man's scope,
With what I most enjoy contented least;
Yet in these thoughts myself almost despising,
Haply I think on thee,—and then my state
(Like to the lark at break of day arising
From sullen earth) sings hymns at heaven's gate;
    For thy sweet love remember'd such wealth brings,
    That then I scorn to change my state with kings.

XXX

When to the sessions of sweet silent thought
I summon up remembrance of things past,
I sigh the lack of many a thing I sought,
And with old woes new wail my dear time's waste:
Then can I drown an eye, unus'd to flow,
For precious friends hid in death's dateless night,
And weep afresh love's long-since-cancell'd woe,
And moan th' expense of many a vanish'd sight:
Then can I grieve at grievances foregone,
And heavily from woe to woe tell o'er
The sad account of fore-bemoaned moan,
Which I new pay as if not paid before.
    But if the while I think on thee, dear friend,
    All losses are restor'd, and sorrows end.

XXXI

Thy bosom is endeared with all hearts,
Which I by lacking have supposed dead;
And there reigns love, and all love's loving parts,
And all those friends which I thought buried.
How many a holy and obsequious tear
Hath dear-religious love stol'n from mine eye,
As interest of the dead, which now appear
But things remov'd, that hidden in thee lie!
Thou art the grave where buried love doth live,
Hung with the trophies of my lovers gone,
Who all their parts of me to thee did give;
That due of many now is thine alone:
    Their images I lov'd I view in thee,
    And thou, all they, hast all-the-all of me.

XXXII

If thou survive my well-contented day,
When that churl Death my bones with dust shall cover,
And shalt by fortune once more re-survey
These poor rude lines of thy deceased lover,
Compare them with the bettering of the time;
And though they be outstripp'd by every pen,
Reserve them for my love, not for their rhyme,
Exceeded by the height of happier men.
O, then vouchsafe me but this loving thought,—
"Had my friend's Muse grown with this growing age,
A dearer birth than this his love had brought,
To march in ranks of better equipage:
      But since he died, and poets better prove,
      Theirs for their style I'll read, his for his love."

XXXIII

Full many a glorious morning have I seen
Flatter the mountain-tops with sovereign eye,
Kissing with golden face the meadows green,
Gilding pale streams with heavenly alchemy;
Anon permit the basest clouds to ride
With ugly rack on his celestial face,
And from the forlorn world his visage hide,
Stealing unseen to west with this disgrace:
Even so my sun one early morn did shine
With all-triumphant splendour on my brow;
But, out, alack! he was but one hour mine,
The region cloud hath mask'd him from me now.
      Yet him for this my love no whit disdaineth;
      Suns of the world may stain when heaven's sun staineth.

XXXIV

Why didst thou promise such a beauteous day,
And make me travel forth without my cloak,
To let base clouds o'ertake me in my way,
Hiding thy bravery in their rotten smoke?
'Tis not enough that through the cloud thou break,
To dry the rain on my storm-beaten face,
For no man well of such a salve can speak,
That heals the wound, and cures not the disgrace:
Nor can thy shame give physic to my grief;
Though thou repent, yet I have still the loss:
Th' offender's sorrow lends but weak relief
To him that bears the strong offence's cross.
  Ah, but those tears are pearl which thy love sheds,
  And they are rich, and ransom all ill deeds.

XXXV

No more be griev'd at that which thou hast done:
Roses have thorns, and silver fountains mud;
Clouds and eclipses stain both moon and sun,
And loathsome canker lives in sweetest bud.
All men make faults, and even I in this,
Authorizing thy trespass with compare,
Myself corrupting, salving thy amiss,
Excusing thy sins more than thy sins are:
For to thy sensual fault I bring in sense,—
Thy adverse party is thy advocate,—
And 'gainst myself a lawful plea commence:
Such civil war is in my love and hate,
  That I an accessory needs must be
  To that sweet thief which sourly robs from me.

XXXVI

Let me confess that we two must be twain,
Although our undivided loves are one;
So shall those blots that do with me remain,
Without thy help, by me be borne alone.
In our two loves there is but one respect,
Though in our lives a separable spite,
Which though it alter not love's sole effect,
Yet doth it steal sweet hours from love's delight.
I may not evermore acknowledge thee,
Lest my bewailed guilt should do thee shame;
Nor thou with public kindness honour me,
Unless thou take that honour from thy name:
    But do not so; I love thee in such sort,
    As, thou being mine, mine is thy good report.

XXXVII

As a decrepit father takes delight
To see his active child do deeds of youth,
So I, made lame by fortune's dearest spite,
Take all my comfort of thy worth and truth;
For whether beauty, birth, or wealth, or wit,
Or any of these all, or all, or more,
Entitled in thy parts do crowned sit,
I make my love engrafted to this store:
So then I am not lame, poor, nor despis'd,
Whilst that this shadow doth such substance give,
That I in thy abundance am suffic'd,
And by a part of all thy glory live.
    Look what is best, that best I wish in thee;
    This wish I have; then ten times happy me!

XXXVIII

How can my Muse want subject to invent,
While thou dost breathe, that pour'st into my verse
Thine own sweet argument, too excellent
For every vulgar paper to rehearse?
O, give thyself the thanks, if aught in me
Worthy perusal stand against thy sight;
For who's so dumb that cannot write to thee,
When thou thyself dost give invention light?
Be thou the tenth Muse, ten times more in worth
Than those old nine which rhymers invocate;
And he that calls on thee, let him bring forth
Eternal numbers to out-live long date.
    If my slight Muse do please these curious days,
    The pain be mine, but thine shall be the praise.

XXXIX

O, how thy worth with manners may I sing,
When thou art all the better part of me?
What can mine own praise to mine own self bring?
And what is 't but mine own, when I praise thee?
Even for this let us divided live,
And our dear love lose name of single one,
That by this separation I may give
That due to thee, which thou deserv'st alone.
O absence, what a torment wouldst thou prove,
Were it not thy sour leisure gave sweet leave
To entertain the time with thoughts of love,—
Which time and thoughts so sweetly doth deceive,—
    And that thou teachest how to make one twain,
    By praising him here who doth hence remain!

XL

Take all my loves, my love, yea, take them all;
What hast thou then more than thou hadst before?
No love, my love, that thou mayst true love call;
All mine was thine before thou hadst this more.
Then, if for my love thou my love receivest,
I cannot blame thee for my love thou usest;
But yet be blam'd, if thou thyself deceivest
By wilful taste of what thyself refusest.
I do forgive thy robbery, gentle thief,
Although thou steal thee all my poverty;
And yet, love knows, it is a greater grief
To bear love's wrong, than hate's known injury.
> Lascivious grace, in whom all ill well shows,
> Kill me with spites; yet we must not be foes.

XLI

Those pretty wrongs that liberty commits
When I am sometime absent from thy heart,
Thy beauty and thy years full well befits,
For still temptation follows where thou art.
Gentle thou art, and therefore to be won,
Beauteous thou art, therefore to be assail'd;
And when a woman woos, what woman's son
Will sourly leave her till she have prevail'd?
Ah me! but yet thou mightst my seat forbear,
And chide thy beauty and thy straying youth,
Who lead thee in their riot even there
Where thou art forc'd to break a two-fold truth,—
> Hers, by thy beauty tempting her to thee,
> Thine, by thy beauty being false to me.

XLII

That thou hast her, it is not all my grief,
And yet it may be said I lov'd her dearly;
That she hath thee, is of my wailing chief,
A loss in love that touches me more nearly.
Loving offenders, thus I will excuse ye:—
Thou dost love her, because thou know'st I love her;
And for my sake even so doth she abuse me,
Suffering my friend for my sake to approve her.
If I lose thee, my loss is my love's gain,
And losing her, my friend hath found that loss;
Both find each other, and I lose both twain,
And both for my sake lay on me this cross:
    But here 's the joy,—my friend and I are one;
    Sweet flattery!—then she loves but me alone.

XLIII

When most I wink, then do mine eyes best see,
For all the day they view things unrespected;
But when I sleep, in dreams they look on thee,
And, darkly bright, are bright in dark directed.
Then thou, whose shadow shadows doth make bright,
How would thy shadow's form form happy show,
To the clear day with thy much clearer light,
When to unseeing eyes thy shade shines so!
How would, I say, mine eyes be blessed made
By looking on thee in the living day,
When in dead night thy fair imperfect shade
Through heavy sleep on sightless eyes doth stay!
    All days are nights to see till I see thee,
    And nights, bright days when dreams do show thee me.

XLIV

If the dull substance of my flesh were thought,
Injurious distance should not stop my way;
For then, despite of space, I would be brought
From limits far remote, where thou dost stay.
No matter then although my foot did stand
Upon the farthest earth remov'd from thee;
For nimble thought can jump both sea and land,
As soon as think the place where he would be.
But, ah! thought kills me, that I am not thought,
To leap large lengths of miles when thou art gone,
But that, so much of earth and water wrought,
I must attend time's leisure with my moan;
    Receiving nought by elements so slow
    But heavy tears, badges of either's woe.

XLV

The other two, slight air and purging fire,
Are both with thee, wherever I abide;
The first my thought, the other my desire,
These present-absent with swift motion slide.
For when these quicker elements are gone
In tender embassy of love to thee,
My life, being made of four, with two alone
Sinks down to death, oppress'd with melancholy;
Until life's composition be recur'd
By those swift messengers return'd from thee,
Who even but now come back again, assur'd
Of thy fair health, recounting it to me:
    This told, I joy; but then no longer glad,
    I send them back again, and straight grow sad.

XLVI

Mine eye and heart are at a mortal war,
How to divide the conquest of thy sight;
Mine eye my heart thy picture's sight would bar,
My heart mine eye the freedom of that right.
My heart doth plead that thou in him dost lie,—
A closet never pierc'd with crystal eyes,—
But the defendant doth that plea deny,
And says in him thy fair appearance lies.
To 'cide this title is impannelled
A quest of thoughts, all tenants to the heart;
And by their verdict is determined
The clear eye's moiety and the dear heart's part:
    As thus,—mine eye's due is thine outward part,
    And my heart's right thine inward love of heart.

XLVII

Betwixt mine eye and heart a league is took,
And each doth good turns now unto the other:
When that mine eye is famish'd for a look,
Or heart in love with sighs himself doth smother,
With my love's picture then my eye doth feast,
And to the painted banquet bids my heart;
Another time mine eye is my heart's guest,
And in his thoughts of love doth share a part:
So, either by thy picture or my love,
Thyself away art present still with me;
For thou not farther than my thoughts canst move,
And I am still with them, and they with thee;
    Or, if they sleep, thy picture in my sight
    Awakes my heart to heart's and eye's delight.

XLVIII

How careful was I, when I took my way,
Each trifle under truest bars to thrust,
That to my use it might unused stay
From hands of falsehood, in sure wards of trust
But thou, to whom my jewels trifles are,
Most worthy comfort, now my greatest grief,
Thou, best of dearest, and mine only care,
Art left the prey of every vulgar thief.
Thee have I not lock'd up in any chest,
Save where thou art not, though I feel thou art,
Within the gentle closure of my breast,
From whence at pleasure thou mayst come and part;
 And even thence thou wilt be stol'n I fear,
 For truth proves thievish for a prize so dear.

XLIX

Against that time, if ever that time come,
When I shall see thee frown on my defects,
Whenas thy love hath cast his utmost sum,
Call'd to that audit by advis'd respects;
Against that time, when thou shalt strangely pass,
And scarcely greet me with that sun, thine eye,
When love, converted from the thing it was,
Shall reasons find of settled gravity,—
Against that time do I ensconce me here
Within the knowledge of mine own desert,
And this my hand against myself uprear,
To guard the lawful reasons on thy part:
 To leave poor me thou hast the strength of laws,
 Since why to love I can allege no cause.

L

How heavy do I journey on the way,
When what I seek,—my weary travel's end,—
Doth teach that ease and that repose to say,
"Thus far the miles are measur'd from thy friend!"
The beast that bears me, tired with my woe,
Plods dully on, to bear that weight in me,
As if by some instinct the wretch did know
His rider lov'd not speed, being made from thee:
The bloody spur cannot provoke him on
That sometimes anger thrusts into his hide,
Which heavily he answers with a groan,
More sharp to me than spurring to his side;
    For that same groan doth put this in my mind,—
    My grief lies onward, and my joy behind.

LI

Thus can my love excuse the slow offence
Of my dull bearer when from thee I speed:
From where thou art why should I haste me thence?
Till I return, of posting is no need.
O, what excuse will my poor beast then find,
When swift extremity can seem but slow?
Then should I spur, though mounted on the wind,
In winged speed no motion shall I know:
Then can no horse with my desire keep pace;
Therefore desire, of perfect'st love being made,
Shall neigh,—no dull flesh,—in his fiery race;
But love, for love, thus shall excuse my jade,—
    Since from thee going he went wilful-slow,
    Towards thee I'll run, and give him leave to go.

LII

So am I as the rich, whose blessed key
Can bring him to his sweet up-locked treasure,
The which he will not every hour survey,
For blunting the fine point of seldom pleasure.
Therefore are feasts so solemn and so rare,
Since, seldom coming, in the long year set,
Like stones of worth they thinly placed are,
Or captain jewels in the carcanet.
So is the time that keeps you, as my chest,
Or as the wardrobe which the robe doth hide,
To make some special instant special-blest,
By new unfolding his imprison'd pride.
    Blessed are you, whose worthiness gives scope,
    Being had, to triumph, being lack'd, to hope.

LIII

What is your substance, whereof are you made,
That millions of strange shadows on you tend?
Since every one hath, every one, one shade,
And you, but one, can every shadow lend.
Describe Adonis, and the counterfeit
Is poorly imitated after you;
On Helen's cheek all art of beauty set,
And you in Grecian tires are painted new:
Speak of the spring, and foison of the year;
The one doth shadow of your beauty show,
The other as your bounty doth appear;
And you in every blessed shape we know.
    In all external grace you have some part,
    But you like none, none you, for constant heart.

LIV

O, how much more doth beauty beauteous seem
By that sweet ornament which truth doth give!
The rose looks fair, but fairer we it deem
For that sweet odour which doth in it live.
The canker-blooms have full as deep a dye
As the perfumed tincture of the roses,
Hang on such thorns, and play as wantonly
When summer's breath their masked buds discloses:
But, for their virtue only is their show,
They live unwoo'd, and unrespected fade;
Die to themselves. Sweet roses do not so;
Of their sweet deaths are sweetest odours made:
    And so of you, beauteous and lovely youth,
    When that shall fade, by verse distils your truth.

LV

Not marble, not the gilded monuments
Of princes, shall outlive this powerful rhyme;
But you shall shine more bright in these contents
Than unswept stone, besmear'd with sluttish time.
When wasteful war shall statues overturn,
And broils root out the work of masonry,
Nor Mars his sword nor war's quick fire shall burn
The living record of your memory.
'Gainst death and all-oblivious enmity
Shall you pace forth; your praise shall still find room,
Even in the eyes of all posterity
That wear this world out to the ending doom.
    So, till the judgment that yourself arise,
    You live in this, and dwell in lovers' eyes.

LVI

Sweet love, renew thy force; be it not said
Thy edge should blunter be than appetite,
Which but to-day by feeding is allay'd,
To-morrow sharpen'd in his former might:
So, love, be thou: although to-day thou fill
Thy hungry eyes, even till they wink with fullness,
To-morrow see again, and do not kill
The spirit of love with a perpetual dullness.
Let this sad interim like the ocean be
Which parts the shore, where two contracted-new
Come daily to the banks, that, when they see
Return of love, more blest may be the view;
  Or call it winter, which, being full of care,
  Makes summer's welcome thrice more wish'd, more rare.

LVII

Being your slave, what should I do but tend
Upon the hours and times of your desire?
I have no precious time at all to spend,
Nor services to do, till you require.
Nor dare I chide the world-without-end hour,
Whilst I, my sovereign, watch the clock for you,
Nor think the bitterness of absence sour,
When you have bid your servant once adieu;
Nor dare I question with my jealous thought
Where you may be, or your affairs suppose,
But, like a sad slave, stay and think of nought
Save, where you are how happy you make those.
  So true a fool is love, that in your will,
  Though you do anything, he thinks no ill.

LVIII

That god forbid that made me first your slave,
I should in thought control your times of pleasure,
Or at your hand th' account of hours to crave,
Being your vassal, bound to stay your leisure!
O, let me suffer, being at your beck,
Th' imprison'd absence of your liberty;
And patience, tame to sufferance, bide each check,
Without accusing you of injury.
Be where you list, your charter is so strong,
That you yourself may privilege your time:
Do what you will, to you it doth belong
Yourself to pardon of self-doing crime.
    I am to wait, though waiting so be hell;
    Not blame your pleasure, be it ill or well.

LIX

If there be nothing new, but that which is
Hath been before, how are our brains beguil'd,
Which, labouring for invention, bear amiss
The second burden of a former child!
O, that record could with a backward look,
Even of five hundred courses of the sun,
Show me your image in some antique book,
Since mind at first in character was done!
That I might see what the old world could say
To this composed wonder of your frame;
Whether we are mended, or whêr better they,
Or whether revolution be the same.
    O, sure I am, the wits of former days
    To subjects worse have given admiring praise!

LX

Like as the waves make towards the pebbled shore,
So do our minutes hasten to their end;
Each changing place with that which goes before,
In sequent toil all forwards do contend.
Nativity, once in the main of light,
Crawls to maturity, wherewith being crown'd,
Crooked eclipses 'gainst his glory fight,
And Time, that gave, doth now his gift confound.
Time doth transfix the flourish set on youth,
And delves the parallels in beauty's brow;
Feeds on the rarities of nature's truth,
And nothing stands but for his scythe to mow:
    And yet, to times in hope my verse shall stand,
    Praising thy worth, despite his cruel hand.

LXI

Is it thy will thy image should keep open
My heavy eyelids to the weary night?
Dost thou desire my slumbers should be broken
While shadows like to thee do mock my sight?
Is it thy spirit that thou send'st from thee
So far from home into my deeds to pry,
To find out shames and idle hours in me,
The scope and tenour of thy jealousy?
O, no! thy love, though much, is not so great;
It is my love that keeps mine eye awake;
Mine own true love that doth my rest defeat,
To play the watchman ever for thy sake:
    For thee watch I whilst thou dost wake else where,
    From me far off, with others all-too-near.

LXII

Sin of self-love possesseth all mine eye,
And all my soul, and all my every part;
And for this sin there is no remedy,
It is so grounded inward in my heart.
Methinks no face so gracious is as mine,
No shape so true, no truth of such account;
And for myself mine own worth do define,
As I all other in all worths surmount.
But when my glass shows me myself indeed,
Beated and chapp'd with tann'd antiquity,
Mine own self-love quite contrary I read;
Self so self-loving were iniquity.
    'Tis thee (myself) that for myself I praise,
    Painting my age with beauty of thy days.

LXIII

Against my love shall be, as I am now,
With Time's injurious hand crush'd and o'erworn;
When hours have drain'd his blood, and fill'd his brow
With lines and wrinkles; when his youthful morn
Hath travell'd on to age's steepy night;
And all those beauties whereof now he's king
Are vanishing or vanish'd out of sight,
Stealing away the treasure of his spring;
For such a time do I now fortify
Against confounding age's cruel knife,
That he shall never cut from memory
My sweet love's beauty, though my lover's life:
    His beauty shall in these black lines be seen,
    And they shall live, and he in them, still green.

LXIV

When I have seen by Time's fell hand defac'd
The rich-proud cost of outworn buried age;
When sometime lofty towers I see down-raz'd,
And brass eternal slave to mortal rage;
When I have seen the hungry ocean gain
Advantage on the kingdom of the shore,
And the firm soil win of the wat'ry main,
Increasing store with loss, and loss with store;
When I have seen such interchange of state,
Or state itself confounded to decay;
Ruin hath taught me thus to ruminate,—
That Time will come and take my love away.
    This thought is as a death, which cannot choose
    But weep to have that which it fears to lose.

LXV

Since brass, nor stone, nor earth, nor boundless sea,
But sad mortality o'er-sways their power,
How with this rage shall beauty hold a plea,
Whose action is no stronger than a flower?
O, how shall summer's honey breath hold out
Against the wreckful siege of battering days,
When rocks impregnable are not so stout,
Nor gates of steel so strong, but Time decays?
O fearful meditation! where, alack!
Shall Time's best jewel from Time's chest lie hid?
Or what strong hand can hold his swift foot back?
Or who his spoil of beauty can forbid?
    O, none, unless this miracle have might,
    That in black ink my love may still shine bright.

LXVI

Tir'd with all these, for restful death I cry,—
As, to behold desert a beggar born,
And needy nothing trimm'd in jollity,
And purest faith unhappily forsworn,
And gilded honour shamefully misplac'd,
And maiden virtue rudely strumpeted,
And right perfection wrongfully disgrac'd,
And strength by limping sway disabled,
And art made tongue-tied by authority,
And folly, doctor-like, controlling skill,
And simple truth miscall'd simplicity,
And captive good attending captain ill:—
    Tir'd with all these, from these would I be gone,
    Save that, to die, I leave my love alone.

LXVII

Ah, wherefore with infection should he live,
And with his presence grace impiety,
That sin by him advantage should achieve,
And lace itself with his society?
Why should false painting imitate his cheek,
And steal dead seeing of his living hue?
Why should poor beauty indirectly seek
Roses of shadow, since his rose is true?
Why should he live, now Nature bankrupt is,
Beggar'd of blood to blush through lively veins?
For she hath no exchequer now but his,
And, proud of many, lives upon his gains.
    O, him she stores, to show what wealth she had
    In days long since, before these last so bad.

LXVIII

Thus is his cheek the map of days outworn,
When beauty liv'd and died as flowers do now,
Before these bastard signs of fair were born,
Or durst inhabit on a living brow;
Before the golden tresses of the dead,
The right of sepulchres, were shorn away,
To live a second life on second head;
Ere beauty's dead fleece made another gay:
In him those holy antique hours are seen,
Without all ornament, itself, and true,
Making no summer of another's green,
Robbing no old to dress his beauty new;
 And him as for a map doth Nature store,
 To show false Art what beauty was of yore.

LXIX

Those parts of thee that the world's eye doth view
Want nothing that the thought of hearts can mend;
All tongues, the voice of souls, give thee that due,
Uttering bare truth, even so as foes commend.
Thine outward thus with outward praise is crown'd;
But those same tongues that give thee so thine own,
In other accents do this praise confound,
By seeing farther than the eye hath shown.
They look into the beauty of thy mind,
And that, in guess, they measure by thy deeds;
Then, churls, their thoughts, although their eyes were kind,
To thy fair flower add the rank smell of weeds:
 But why thy odour matcheth not thy show,
 The solve is this,—that thou dost common grow.

LXX

That thou art blam'd shall not be thy defect,
For slander's mark was ever yet the fair;
The ornament of beauty is suspect,
A crow that flies in heaven's sweetest air.
So thou be good, slander doth but approve
Thy worth the greater, being woo'd of time;
For canker vice the sweetest buds doth love,
And thou present'st a pure unstained prime.
Thou hast pass'd by the ambush of young days,
Either not assail'd, or victor being charg'd;
Yet this thy praise cannot be so thy praise,
To tie up envy evermore enlarg'd:
    If some suspect of ill mask'd not thy show,
    Then thou alone kingdoms of hearts shouldst owe.

LXXI

No longer mourn for me when I am dead
Than you shall hear the surly sullen bell
Give warning to the world that I am fled
From this vile world, with vilest worms to dwell:
Nay, if you read this line, remember not
The hand that writ it; for I love you so,
That I in your sweet thoughts would be forgot,
If thinking on me then should make you woe.
Oh, if, I say, you look upon this verse
When I perhaps compounded am with clay,
Do not so much as my poor name rehearse;
But let your love even with my life decay;
    Lest the wise world should look into your moan,
    And mock you with me after I am gone.

LXXII

O, lest the world should task you to recite
What merit liv'd in me that you should love,
After my death, dear love, forget me quite;
For you in me can nothing worthy prove
Unless you would devise some virtuous lie,
To do more for me than mine own desert,
And hang more praise upon deceased I
Than niggard truth would willingly impart:
O, lest your true love may seem false in this,
That you for love speak well of me untrue,
My name be buried where my body is,
And live no more to shame nor me nor you.
    For I am sham'd by that which I bring forth,
    And so should you, to love things nothing worth.

LXXIII

That time of year thou mayst in me behold
When yellow leaves, or none, or few, do hang
Upon those boughs which shake against the cold,
Bare ruin'd choirs, where late the sweet birds sang.
In me thou see'st the twilight of such day
As after sunset fadeth in the west;
Which by and by black night doth take away,
Death's second self, that seals up all in rest.
In me thou see'st the glowing of such fire,
That on the ashes of his youth doth lie,
As the death-bed whereon it must expire,
Consum'd with that which it was nourish'd by.
    This thou perceiv'st, which makes thy love more strong,
    To love that well which thou must leave ere long.

LXXIV

But be contented: when that fell arrest
Without all bail shall carry me away,
My life hath in this line some interest,
Which for memorial still with thee shall stay.
When thou reviewest this, thou dost review
The very part was consecrate to thee:
The earth can have but earth, which is his due;
My spirit is thine, the better part of me:
So, then, thou hast but lost the dregs of life,
The prey of worms, my body being dead;
The coward conquest of a wretch's knife,
Too base of thee to be remembered.
    The worth of that, is that which it contains,
    And that is this, and this with thee remains.

LXXV

So are you to my thoughts as food to life,
Or as sweet-season'd showers are to the ground;
And for the peace of you I hold such strife
As 'twixt a miser and his wealth is found;
Now proud as an enjoyer, and anon
Doubting the filching age will steal his treasure;
Now counting best to be with you alone,
Then better'd that the world may see my pleasure:
Sometime all full with feasting on your sight,
And by and by clean starved for a look;
Possessing or pursuing no delight,
Save what is had or must from you be took.
    Thus do I pine and surfeit day by day,
    Or gluttoning on all, or all away.

LXXVI

Why is my verse so barren of new pride,
So far from variation or quick change?
Why, with the time, do I not glance aside
To new-found methods and to compounds strange?
Why write I still all one, ever the same,
And keep invention in a noted weed,
That every word doth almost tell my name,
Showing their birth, and where they did proceed?
O, know, sweet love, I always write of you,
And you and love are still my argument;
So all my best is dressing old words new,
Spending again what is already spent:
    For as the sun is daily new and old,
    So is my love still telling what is told.

LXXVII

Thy glass will show thee how thy beauties wear,
Thy dial how thy precious minutes waste;
The vacant leaves thy mind's imprint will bear,
And of this book this learning mayst thou taste.
The wrinkles which thy glass will truly show,
Of mouthed graves will give thee memory;
Thou by thy dial's shady stealth mayst know
Time's thievish progress to eternity.
Look, what thy memory cannot contain,
Commit to these waste blanks, and thou shalt find
Those children nurs'd, deliver'd from thy brain,
To take a new acquaintance of thy mind.
    These offices, so oft as thou wilt look,
    Shall profit thee, and much enrich thy book.

LXXVIII

So oft have I invok'd thee for my Muse,
And found such fair assistance in my verse,
As every alien pen hath got my use,
And under thee their poesy disperse.
Thine eyes, that taught the dumb on high to sing,
And heavy ignorance aloft to fly,
Have added feathers to the learned's wing,
And given grace a double majesty.
Yet be most proud of that which I compile,
Whose influence is thine, and born of thee:
In others' works thou dost but mend the style,
And arts with thy sweet graces graced be;
    But thou art all my art, and dost advance
    As high as learning my rude ignorance.

LXXIX

Whilst I alone did call upon thy aid,
My verse alone had all thy gentle grace;
But now my gracious numbers are decay'd,
And my sick Muse doth give another place.
I grant, sweet love, thy lovely argument
Deserves the travail of a worthier pen;
Yet what of thee thy poet doth invent,
He robs thee of, and pays it thee again.
He lends thee virtue, and he stole that word
From thy behaviour; beauty doth he give,
And found it in thy cheek; he can afford
No praise to thee but what in thee doth live.
    Then thank him not for that which he doth say,
    Since what he owes thee thou thyself dost pay.

LXXX

O, how I faint when I of you do write,
Knowing a better spirit doth use your name,
And in the praise thereof spends all his might,
To make me tongue-tied, speaking of your fame!
But since your worth, wide as the ocean is,
The humble as the proudest sail doth bear,
My saucy bark, inferior far to his,
On your broad main doth wilfully appear.
Your shallowest help will hold me up afloat,
Whilst he upon your soundless deep doth ride;
Or, being wreck'd, I am a worthless boat,
He of tall building and of goodly pride:
    Then if he thrive, and I be cast away,
    The worst was this,—my love was my decay.

LXXXI

Or I shall live your epitaph to make,
Or you survive when I in earth am rotten;
From hence your memory death cannot take,
Although in me each part will be forgotten.
Your name from hence immortal life shall have,
Though I, once gone, to all the world must die:
The earth can yield me but a common grave,
When you entombed in men's eyes shall lie.
Your monument shall be my gentle verse,
Which eyes not yet created shall o'er-read;
And tongues to be your being shall rehearse,
When all the breathers of this world are dead;
    You still shall live,—such virtue hath my pen,—
    Where breath most breathes,—even in the mouths of men.

LXXXII

I grant thou wert not married to my Muse,
And therefore mayst without attaint o'erlook
The dedicated words which writers use
Of their fair subject, blessing every book.
Thou art as fair in knowledge as in hue,
Finding thy worth a limit past my praise;
And therefore art enforc'd to seek anew
Some fresher stamp of the time-bettering days.
And do so, love; yet when they have devis'd
What strained touches rhetoric can lend,
Thou truly fair wert truly sympathiz'd
In true-plain words, by thy true-telling friend;
    And their gross painting might be better us'd
    Where cheeks need blood,—in thee it is abus'd.

LXXXIII

I never saw that you did painting need,
And therefore to your fair no painting set;
I found, or thought I found, you did exceed
The barren tender of a poet's debt:
And therefore have I slept in your report,
That you yourself, being extant, well might show
How far a modern quill doth come too short,
Speaking of worth, what worth in you doth grow.
This silence for my sin you did impute,
Which shall be most my glory, being dumb;
For I impair not beauty, being mute,
When others would give life, and bring a tomb.
    There lives more life in one of your fair eyes
    Than both your poets can in praise devise.

LXXXIV

Who is it that says most? which can say more
Than this rich praise,—that you alone are you?
In whose confine immured is the store
Which should example where your equal grew?
Lean penury within that pen doth dwell,
That to his subject lends not some small glory;
But he that writes of you, if he can tell
That you are you, so dignifies his story.
Let him but copy what in you is writ,
Not making worse what nature made so clear,
And such a counterpart shall fame his wit,
Making his style admired every where.
    You to your beauteous blessings add a curse,
    Being fond on praise, which makes your praises worse.

LXXXV

My tongue-tied Muse in manners holds her still,
While comments of your praise, richly compil'd,
Reserve their character with golden quill,
And precious phrase by all the Muses fil'd.
I think good thoughts, whilst others write good words,
And, like unletter'd clerk, still cry "Amen"
To every hymn that able spirit affords,
In polish'd form of well-refined pen.
Hearing you prais'd, I say, "'Tis so, 'tis true,"
And to the most of praise add something more;
But that is in my thought, whose love to you,
Though words come hindmost, holds his rank before.
    Then others for the breath of words respect,
    Me for my dumb thoughts, speaking in effect.

LXXXVI

Was it the proud full sail of his great verse,
Bound for the prize of all-too-precious you,
That did my ripe thoughts in my brain inhearse,
Making their tomb the womb wherein they grew?
Was it his spirit, by spirits taught to write
Above a mortal pitch, that struck me dead?
No, neither he, nor his compeers by night
Giving him aid, my verse astonished.
He, nor that affable-familiar ghost
Which nightly gulls him with intelligence,
As victors, of my silence cannot boast;
I was not sick of any fear from thence,
    But when your countenance fil'd up his line,
    Then lack'd I matter; that enfeebled mine.

LXXXVII

Farewell! thou art too dear for my possessing,
And like enough thou know'st thy estimate:
The charter of thy worth gives thee releasing;
My bonds in thee are all determinate.
For how do I hold thee but by thy granting?
And for that riches where is my deserving?
The cause of this fair gift in me is wanting,
And so my patent back again is swerving.
Thyself thou gav'st, thy own worth then not knowing,
Or me to whom thou gav'st, else mistaking;
So thy great gift, upon misprision growing,
Comes home again, on better judgment making.
    Thus have I had thee, as a dream doth flatter,
    In sleep a king, but waking no such matter.

LXXXVIII

When thou shalt be dispos'd to set me light,
And place my merit in the eye of Scorn,
Upon thy side against myself I'll fight,
And prove thee virtuous, though thou art forsworn.
With mine own weakness being best acquainted,
Upon thy part I can set down a story
Of faults conceal'd, wherein I am attainted;
That thou, in losing me, shalt win much glory:
And I by this will be a gainer too;
For bending all my loving thoughts on thee,
The injuries that to myself I do,
Doing thee vantage, double-vantage me.
    Such is my love, to thee I so belong,
    That for thy right myself will bear all wrong.

LXXXIX

Say that thou didst forsake me for some fault,
And I will comment upon that offence;
Speak of my lameness, and I straight will halt,
Against thy reasons making no defence.
Thou canst not, love, disgrace me half so ill,
To set a form upon desired change,
As I'll myself disgrace: knowing thy will,
I will acquaintance strangle, and look strange;
Be absent from thy walks; and in my tongue
Thy sweet-beloved name no more shall dwell,
Lest I, too much profane, should do it wrong,
And haply of our old acquaintance tell.
    For thee, against myself I'll vow debate,
    For I must ne'er love him whom thou dost hate.

XC

Then hate me when thou wilt; if ever, now;
Now, while the world is bent my deeds to cross,
Join with the spite of fortune, make me bow,
And do not drop in for an after-loss:
Ah, do not, when my heart hath scap'd this sorrow,
Come in the rearward of a conquer'd woe!
Give not a windy night a rainy morrow,
To linger out a purpos'd overthrow.
If thou wilt leave me, do not leave me last,
When other petty griefs have done their spite,
But in the onset come; so shall I taste
At first the very worst of fortune's might;
    And other strains of woe, which now seem woe,
    Compar'd with loss of thee will not seem so.

XCI

Some glory in their birth, some in their skill,
Some in their wealth, some in their body's force;
Some in their garments, though new-fangled ill;
Some in their hawks and hounds, some in their horse;
And every humour hath his adjunct pleasure,
Wherein it finds a joy above the rest:
But these particulars are not my measure;
All these I better in one general best.
Thy love is better than high birth to me,
Richer than wealth, prouder than garments' cost,
Of more delight than hawks or horses be;
And, having thee, of all men's pride I boast:
    Wretched in this alone, that thou mayst take
    All this away, and me most wretched make.

XCII

But do thy worst to steal thyself away,
For term of life thou art assured mine;
And life no longer than thy love will stay,
For it depends upon that love of thine.
Then need I not to fear the worst of wrongs,
When in the least of them my life hath end.
I see a better state to me belongs
Than that which on thy humour doth depend:
Thou canst not vex me with inconstant mind,
Since that my life on thy revolt doth lie.
O, what a happy title do I find,
Happy to have thy love, happy to die!
    But what's so blessed-fair that fears no blot?—
    Thou mayst be false, and yet I know it not:

XCIII

So shall I live, supposing thou art true,
Like a deceived husband; so love's face
May still seem love to me, though alter'd-new;
Thy looks with me, thy heart in other place:
For there can live no hatred in thine eye,
Therefore in that I cannot know thy change.
In many's looks the false heart's history
Is writ, in moods and frowns and wrinkles strange,
But heaven in thy creation did decree
That in thy face sweet love should ever dwell;
Whate'er thy thoughts or thy heart's workings be,
Thy looks should nothing thence but sweetness tell.
    How like Eve's apple doth thy beauty grow,
    If thy sweet virtue answer not thy show!

XCIV

They that have power to hurt and will do none,
That do not do the thing they most do show,
Who, moving others, are themselves as stone,
Unmoved, cold, and to temptation slow;
They rightly do inherit heaven's graces,
And husband nature's riches from expense;
They are the lords and owners of their faces,
Others but stewards of their excellence.
The summer's flower is to the summer sweet,
Though to itself it only live and die;
But if that flower with base infection meet,
The basest weed outbraves his dignity:
    For sweetest things turn sourest by their deeds;
    Lilies that fester smell far worse than weeds.

XCV

How sweet and lovely dost thou make the shame
Which, like a canker in the fragrant rose,
Doth spot the beauty of thy budding name!
O, in what sweets dost thou thy sins enclose!
That tongue that tells the story of thy days,
Making lascivious comments on thy sport,
Cannot dispraise but in a kind of praise;
Naming thy name blesses an ill-report.
O, what a mansion have those vices got
Which for their habitation chose out thee,
Where beauty's veil doth cover every blot,
And all things turn to fair, that eyes can see!
    Take heed, dear heart, of this large privilege;
    The hardest knife ill-us'd doth lose his edge.

XCVI

Some say, thy fault is youth, some, wantonness;
Some say, thy grace is youth and gentle sport;
Both grace and faults are lov'd of more and less:
Thou mak'st faults graces that to thee resort.
As on the finger of a throned queen
The basest jewel will be well esteem'd,
So are those errors that in thee are seen
To truths translated, and for true things deem'd.
How many lambs might the stern wolf betray,
If like a lamb he could his looks translate!
How many gazers mightst thou lead away,
If thou wouldst use the strength of all thy state!
　　But do not so; I love thee in such sort,
　　As, thou being mine, mine is thy good report.

XCVII

How like a winter hath my absence been
From thee, the pleasure of the fleeting year!
What freezings have I felt, what dark days seen!
What old December's bareness everywhere!
And yet this time remov'd was summer's time;
The teeming autumn, big with rich increase,
Bearing the wanton burden of the prime,
Like widow'd wombs after their lords' decease:
Yet this abundant issue seem'd to me
But hope of orphans and unfather'd fruit;
For summer and his pleasures wait on thee,
And, thou away, the very birds are mute;
　　Or, if they sing, 'tis with so dull a cheer,
　　That leaves look pale, dreading the winter's near.

XCVIII

From you have I been absent in the spring,
When proud-pied April, dress'd in all his trim,
Had put a spirit of youth in everything,
That heavy Saturn laugh'd and leap'd with him.
Yet nor the lays of birds, nor the sweet smell
Of different flowers in odour and in hue,
Could make me any summer's story tell,
Or from their proud lap pluck them where they grew:
Nor did I wonder at the lily's white,
Nor praise the deep vermilion in the rose;
They were but sweet, but figures of delight,
Drawn after you,—you pattern of all those.
　　　Yet seem'd it winter still, and, you away,
　　　As with your shadow I with these did play:

XCIX

The forward violet thus did I chide:—
Sweet thief, whence didst thou steal thy sweet that smells,
If not from my love's breath? The purple pride
Which on thy soft cheek for complexion dwells,
In my love's veins thou hast too grossly dy'd.
The lily I condemned for thy hand,
And buds of marjoram had stol'n thy hair:
The roses fearfully on thorns did stand,
One blushing shame, another white despair;
A third, nor red nor white, had stol'n of both,
And to his robbery had annex'd thy breath;
But, for his theft, in pride of all his growth
A vengeful canker eat him up to death.
　　　More flowers I noted, yet I none could see,
　　　But sweet or colour it had stol'n from thee.

C

Where art thou, Muse, that thou forgett'st so long
To speak of that which gives thee all thy might?
Spend'st thou thy fury on some worthless song,
Darkening thy power, to lend base subjects light?
Return, forgetful Muse, and straight redeem
In gentle numbers time so idly spent;
Sing to the ear that doth thy lays esteem
And gives thy pen both skill and argument.
Rise, resty Muse, my love's sweet face survey,
If Time have any wrinkle graven there;
If any, be a satire to decay,
And make Time's spoils despised everywhere.
      Give my love fame faster than Time wastes life;
      So thou prevent'st his scythe and crooked knife.

CI

O, truant Muse, what shall be thy amends
For thy neglect of truth in beauty dy'd?
Both truth and beauty on my love depends;
So dost thou too, and therein dignified.
Make answer, Muse: wilt thou not haply say,
"Truth needs no colour with his colour fix'd;
Beauty no pencil, beauty's truth to lay;
But best is best, if never intermix'd?"—
Because he needs no praise, wilt thou be dumb?
Excuse not silence so; for 't lies in thee
To make him much outlive a gilded tomb,
And to be prais'd of ages yet to be.
      Then do thy office, Muse; I teach thee how
      To make him seem long hence as he shows now.

CII

My love is strengthen'd, though more weak in seeming;
I love not less, though less the show appear;
That love is merchandiz'd whose rich esteeming
The owner's tongue doth publish everywhere.
Our love was new, and then but in the spring,
When I was wont to greet it with my lays;
As Philomel in summer's front doth sing,
And stops her pipe in growth of riper days:
Not that the summer is less pleasant now
Than when her mournful hymns did hush the night,
But that wild music burdens every bough,
And sweets grown common lose their dear delight.
    Therefore, like her, I sometime hold my tongue,
    Because I would not dull you with my song.

CIII

Alack, what poverty my Muse brings forth,
That having such a scope to show her pride,
The argument, all bare, is of more worth
Than when it hath my added praise beside!
O, blame me not, if I no more can write!
Look in your glass, and there appears a face
That over-goes my blunt invention quite,
Dulling my lines, and doing me disgrace.
Were it not sinful, then, striving to mend,
To mar the subject that before was well?
For to no other pass my verses tend
Than of your graces and your gifts to tell;
    And more, much more, than in your verse can sit,
    Your own glass shows you when you look in it.

CIV

To me, fair friend, you never can be old,
For as you were when first your eye I ey'd,
Such seems your beauty still. Three winters' cold
Have from the forests shook three summers' pride,
Three beauteous springs to yellow autumn turn'd
In process of the seasons have I seen,
Three April perfumes in three hot Junes burn'd,
Since first I saw you fresh, which yet are green.
Ah, yet doth beauty, like a dial-hand,
Steal from his figure, and no pace perceiv'd!
So your sweet hue, which methinks still doth stand,
Hath motion, and mine eye may be deceiv'd:
 For fear of which, hear this, thou age unbred,—
 Ere you were born was beauty's summer dead.

CV

Let not my love be call'd idolatry,
Nor my beloved as an idol show,
Since all alike my songs and praises be
To one, of one, still such, and ever so.
Kind is my love to-day, to-morrow kind,
Still constant in a wondrous excellence;
Therefore my verse to constancy confin'd,
One thing expressing, leaves out difference.
Fair, kind, and true, is all my argument,—
Fair, kind, and true, varying to other words;
And in this change is my invention spent,
Three themes in one, which wondrous scope affords.
 Fair, kind, and true, have often liv'd alone,
 Which three till now never kept seat in one.

CVI

When in the chronicle of wasted time
I see descriptions of the fairest wights,
And beauty making beautiful old rhyme
In praise of ladies dead and lovely knights,
Then in the blazon of sweet beauty's best,
Of hand, of foot, of lip, of eye, of brow,
I see their antique pen would have express'd
Even such a beauty as you master now.
So all their praises are but prophecies
Of this our time, all you prefiguring;
And, for they look'd but with divining eyes,
They had not skill enough your worth to sing:
    For we, which now behold these present days,
    Have eyes to wonder, but lack tongues to praise.

CVII

Not mine own fears, nor the prophetic soul
Of the wide world dreaming on things to come,
Can yet the lease of my true love control,
Suppos'd as forfeit to a confin'd doom.
The mortal moon hath her eclipse endur'd,
And the sad augurs mock their own presage;
Incertainties now crown themselves assur'd,
And peace proclaims olives of endless age.
Now with the drops of this most balmy time
My love looks fresh, and Death to me subscribes,
Since, spite of him, I'll live in this poor rhyme,
While he insults o'er dull and speechless tribes:
    And thou in this shalt find thy monument,
    When tyrants' crests and tombs of brass are spent.

CVIII

What's in the brain, that ink may character,
Which hath not figur'd to thee my true spirit?
What's new to speak, what new to register,
That may express my love, or thy dear merit?
Nothing, sweet boy; but yet, like prayers divine,
I must each day say o'er the very same;
Counting no old thing old, thou mine, I thine,
Even as when first I hallow'd thy fair name.
So that eternal love in love's fresh case
Weighs not the dust and injury of age,
Nor gives to necessary wrinkles place,
But makes antiquity for aye his page;
    Finding the first conceit of love there bred,
    Where time and outward form would show it dead.

CIX

O, never say that I was false of heart,
Though absence seem'd my flame to qualify!
As easy might I from myself depart,
As from my soul, which in thy breast doth lie:
That is my home of love: if I have rang'd,
Like him that travels, I return again;
Just to the time, not with the time exchang'd,—
So that myself bring water for my stain.
Never believe, though in my nature reign'd
All frailties that besiege all kinds of blood,
That it could so preposterously be stain'd,
To leave for nothing all thy sum of good;
    For nothing this wide universe I call,
    Save thou, my rose; in it thou art my all.

CX

Alas, 'tis true I have gone here and there,
And made myself a motley to the view,
Gor'd mine own thoughts, sold cheap what is most dear,
Made old offences of affections new.
Most true it is that I have look'd on truth
Askance and strangely; but, by all above,
These blenches gave my heart another youth,
And worse essays prov'd thee my best of love.
Now all is done, have what shall have no end:
Mine appetite I never more will grind
On newer proof, to try an older friend,
A god in love, to whom I am confin'd.
    Then give me welcome, next my heaven the best,
    Even to thy pure and most-most loving breast.

CXI

O, for my sake do you with Fortune chide,
The guilty goddess of my harmful deeds,
That did not better for my life provide,
Than public means, which public manners breeds.
Thence comes it that my name receives a brand;
And almost thence my nature is subdu'd
To what it works in, like the dyer's hand:
Pity me, then, and wish I were renew'd;
Whilst, like a willing patient, I will drink
Potions of eisel, 'gainst my strong infection;
No bitterness that I will bitter think,
Nor double penance, to correct correction.
    Pity me, then, dear friend, and I assure ye,
    Even that your pity is enough to cure me.

CXII

Your love and pity doth th' impression fill
Which vulgar scandal stamp'd upon my brow;
For what care I who calls me well or ill,
So you o'er-green my bad, my good allow?
You are my all-the-world, and I must strive
To know my shames and praises from your tongue;
None else to me, nor I to none alive,
That my steel'd sense' or changes right or wrong.
In so profound abysm I throw all care
Of others' voices, that my adder's sense'
To critic and to flatterer stopped are.
Mark how with my neglect I do dispense:—
      You are so strongly in my purpose bred,
      That all the world besides methinks are dead.

CXIII

Since I left you, mine eye is in my mind;
And that which governs me to go about
Doth part his function, and is partly blind,
Seems seeing, but effectually is out;
For it no form delivers to the heart
Of bird, of flower, or shape, which it doth latch:
Of his quick objects hath the mind no part,
Nor his own vision holds what it doth catch;
For if it see the rud'st or gentlest sight,
The most sweet favour or deformed'st creature,
The mountain or the sea, the day or night,
The crow or dove, it shapes them to your feature:
      Incapable of more, replete with you,
      My most true mind thus maketh mine untrue.

CXIV

Or whether doth my mind, being crown'd with you,
Drink up the monarch's plague, this flattery?
Or whether shall I say, mine eye saith true,
And that your love taught it this alchemy,
To make of monsters and things indigest
Such cherubins as your sweet self resemble,
Creating every bad a perfect best,
As fast as objects to his beams assemble?
O, 'tis the first; 'tis flattery in my seeing,
And my great mind most kingly drinks it up:
Mine eye well knows what with his gust is 'greeing,
And to his palate doth prepare the cup:
 If it be poison'd, 'tis the lesser sin
 That mine eye loves it, and doth first begin.

CXV

Those lines that I before have writ do lie;
Even those that said I could not love you dearer:
Yet then my judgment knew no reason why
My most full flame should afterwards burn clearer.
But reckoning Time, whose million'd accidents
Creep in twixt vows, and change decrees of kings,
Tan sacred beauty, blunt the sharp'st intents,
Divert strong minds to the course of altering things;
Alas, why, fearing of Time's tyranny,
Might I not then say, "Now I love you best,"
When I was certain o'er incertainty,
Crowning the present, doubting of the rest?
 Love is a babe; then might I not say so,
 To give full growth to that which still doth grow?

CXVI

Let me not to the marriage of true minds
Admit impediments. Love is not love
Which alters when it alteration finds,
Or bends with the remover to remove:
O, no! it is an ever-fixed mark,
That looks on tempests, and is never shaken;
It is the star to every wandering bark,
Whose worth's unknown, although his height be taken.
Love's not Time's fool, though rosy lips and cheeks
Within his bending sickle's compass come;
Love alters not with his brief hours and weeks,
But bears it out even to the edge of doom.
    If this be error, and upon me prov'd,
    I never writ, nor no man ever lov'd.

CXVII

Accuse me thus:—that I have scanted all
Wherein I should your great deserts repay;
Forgot upon your dearest love to call,
Whereto all bonds do tie me day by day;
That I have frequent been with unknown minds,
And given to time your own dear-purchas'd right;
That I have hoisted sail to all the winds
Which should transport me farthest from your sight.
Book both my wilfulness and errors down,
And on just proof surmise accumulate;
Bring me within the level of your frown,
But shoot not at me in your waken'd hate;
      Since my appeal says I did strive to prove
      The constancy and virtue of your love.

CXVIII

Like as, to make our appetites more keen,
With eager compounds we our palate urge;
As, to prevent our maladies unseen,
We sicken to shun sickness when we purge;
Even so, being full of your ne'er-cloying sweetness,
To bitter sauces did I frame my feeding;
And, sick of welfare, found a kind of meetness
To be diseas'd, ere that there was true needing.
Thus policy in love, to anticipate
The ills that were not, grew to faults assur'd,
And brought to medicine a healthful state,
Which, rank of goodness, would by ill be cur'd.
But thence I learn, and find the lesson true,
Drugs poison him that so fell sick of you.

CXIX

What potions have I drunk of Siren tears,
Distill'd from limbecs foul as hell within,
Applying fears to hopes, and hopes to fears,
Still losing when I saw myself to win!
What wretched errors hath my heart committed,
Whilst it hath thought itself so blessed never!
How have mine eyes out of their spheres been fitted,
In the distraction of this madding fever!
O, benefit of ill! now I find true
That better is by evil still made better;
And ruin'd love, when it is built anew,
Grows fairer than at first, more strong, far greater.
So I return rebuk'd to my content,
And gain by ill thrice more than I have spent.

CXX

That you were once unkind befriends me now,
And for that sorrow which I then did feel
Needs must I under my transgression bow,
Unless my nerves were brass or hammer'd steel.
For if you were by my unkindness shaken,
As I by yours, you've pass'd a hell of time;
And I, a tyrant, have no leisure taken
To weigh how once I suffer'd in your crime.
O, that our night of woe might have remember'd
My deepest sense, how hard true sorrow hits,
And soon to you, as you to me then, tender'd
The humble salve which wounded bosoms fits!
  But that your trespass now becomes a fee;
  Mine ransoms yours, and yours must ransom me.

CXXI

'Tis better to be vile than vile-esteem'd,
When not to be receives reproach of being,
And the just pleasure lost, which is so deem'd
Not by our feeling, but by others' seeing:
For why should others' false-adulterate eyes
Give salutation to my sportive blood?
Or on my frailties why are frailer spies,
Which in their wills count bad what I think good?
No.—I am that I am; and they that level
At my abuses reckon up their own:
I may be straight, though they themselves be bevel;
By their rank thoughts my deeds must not be shown;
  Unless this general evil they maintain,—
  All men are bad, and in their badness reign.

CXXII

Thy gift, thy tables, are within my brain
Full character'd with lasting memory,
Which shall above that idle rank remain,
Beyond all date, even to eternity:
Or, at the least, so long as brain and heart
Have faculty by nature to subsist;
Till each to raz'd oblivion yield his part
Of thee, thy record never can be miss'd.
That poor retention could not so much hold,
Nor need I tallies thy dear love to score;
Therefore to give them from me was I bold,
To trust those tables that receive thee more:
     To keep an adjunct to remember thee,
     Were to import forgetfulness in me.

CXXIII

No, Time, thou shalt not boast that I do change!
Thy pyramids built up with newer might
To me are nothing novel, nothing strange;
They are but dressings of a former sight.
Our dates are brief, and therefore we admire
What thou dost foist upon us that is old;
And rather make them born to our desire
Than think that we before have heard them told.
Thy registers and thee I both defy,
Not wondering at the present nor the past;
For thy records and what we see do lie,
Made more or less by thy continual haste.
     This I do vow, and this shall ever be,
     I will be true, despite thy scythe and thee.

CXXIV

If my dear love were but the child of state,
It might for Fortune's bastard be unfather'd,
As subject to Time's love or to Time's hate,
Weeds among weeds, or flowers with flowers gather'd.
No, it was builded far from accident;
It suffers not in smiling pomp, nor falls
Under the blow of thralled discontent,
Whereto th' inviting time our fashion calls:
It fears not policy, that heretic,
Which works on leases of short-number'd hours,
But all alone stands hugely politic,
That it nor grows with heat nor drowns with showers.
 To this I witness call the fools of time,
 Which die for goodness, who have liv'd for crime.

CXXV

Were 't aught to me I bore the canopy,
With my extern the outward honouring,
Or laid great bases for eternity,
Which prove more short than waste or ruining?
Have I not seen dwellers on form and favour
Lose all, and more, by paying too much rent,
For compound sweet forgoing simple savour,
Pitiful thrivers, in their gazing spent?
No;—let me be obsequious in thy heart,
And take thou my oblation, poor but free,
Which is not mix'd with seconds, knows no art,
But mutual render, only me for thee.
 Hence, thou suborn'd informer! a true soul
 When most impeach'd stands least in thy control.

CXXVI

O thou, my lovely boy, who in thy power
Dost hold Time's fickle glass, his sickle-hour;
Who hast by waning grown, and therein show'st
Thy lovers withering, as thy sweet self grow'st;
If Nature, sovereign mistress over wrack,
As thou goest onwards, still will pluck thee back,
She keeps thee to this purpose, that her skill
May time disgrace, and wretched minutes kill.
Yet fear her, O thou minion of her pleasure!
She may detain, but not still keep, her treasure:
Her audit, though delay'd, answer'd must be,
And her quietus is to render thee.

CXXVII

In the old age black was not counted fair,
Or if it were, it bore not beauty's name;
But now is black beauty's successive heir,
And beauty slander'd with a bastard shame:
For since each hand hath put on nature's power,
Fairing the foul with art's false-borrow'd face,
Sweet beauty hath no name, no holy bower,
But is profan'd, if not lives in disgrace.
Therefore my mistress' eyes are raven black,
Her eyes so suited; and they mourners seem
At such who, not born fair, no beauty lack,
Slandering creation with a false esteem:
Yet so they mourn, becoming of their woe,
That every tongue says beauty should look so.

CXXVIII

How oft, when thou, my music, music play'st,
Upon that blessed wood whose motion sounds
With thy sweet fingers, when thou gently sway'st
The wiry concord that mine ear confounds,
Do I envý those jacks, that nimble leap
To kiss the tender inward of thy hand,
Whilst my poor lips, which should that harvest reap,
At the wood's boldness by thee blushing stand!
To be so tickled, they would change their state
And situation with those dancing chips,
O'er whom thy fingers walk with gentle gait,
Making dead wood more bless'd than living lips.
　　Since saucy jacks so happy are in this,
　　Give them thy fingers, me thy lips to kiss.

CXXIX

Th' expense of spirit in a waste of shame
Is lust in action; and till action, lust
Is perjur'd, murderous, bloody, full of blame.
Savage, extreme, rude, cruel, not to trust;
Enjoy'd no sooner but despised straight;
Past reason hunted; and no sooner had,
Past reason hated, as a swallow'd bait,
On purpose laid to make the taker mad:
Mad in pursuit, and in possession so;
Had, having, and in quest to have, extreme;
A bliss in proof,—and prov'd, a very woe;
Before, a joy propos'd; behind, a dream.
　　All this the world well knows; yet none knows well
　　To shun the heaven that leads men to this hell.

CXXX

My mistress' eyes are nothing like the sun;
Coral is far more red than her lips' red:
If snow be white, why then her breasts are dun;
If hairs be wires, black wires grow on her head.
I have seen roses, damask'd red and white,
But no such roses see I in her cheeks;
And in some perfumes is there more delight
Than in the breath that from my mistress reeks.
I love to hear her speak,—yet well I know
That music hath a far more pleasing sound;
I grant I never saw a goddess go,—
My mistress, when she walks, treads on the ground:
    And yet, by heaven, I think my love as rare
    As any she belied with false compare!

CXXXI

Thou art as tyrannous, so as thou art,
As those whose beauties proudly make them cruel;
For well thou know'st to my dear-doting heart
Thou art the fairest and most precious jewel.
Yet, in good faith, some say that thee behold,
Thy face hath not the power to make love groan:
To say they err, I dare not be so bold,
Although I swear it to myself alone.
And, to be sure that is not false I swear,
A thousand groans, but thinking on thy face,
One on another's neck, do witness bear
Thy black is fairest in my judgment's place.
    In nothing art thou black save in thy deeds,
    And thence this slander, as I think, proceeds.

CXXXII

Thine eyes I love, and they, as pitying me,
Knowing thy heart torments me with disdain,
Have put on black, and loving mourners be,
Looking with pretty ruth upon my pain.
And truly not the morning sun of heaven
Better becomes the grey cheeks of the east,
Nor that full star that ushers in the even
Doth half that glory to the sober west,
As those two mourning eyes become thy face:
O, let it then as well beseem thy heart
To mourn for me, since mourning doth thee grace,
And suit thy pity like in every part.
 Then will I swear beauty herself is black,
 And all they foul that thy complexion lack.

CXXXIII

Beshrew that heart that makes my heart to groan
For that deep wound it gives my friend and me!
Is 't not enough to torture me alone,
But slave to slavery my sweet'st friend must be?
Me from myself thy cruel eye hath taken,
And my next self thou harder hast engross'd:
Of him, myself, and thee, I am forsaken;
A torment thrice three-fold thus to be cross'd.
Prison my heart in thy steel bosom's ward,
But then my friend's heart let my poor heart bail;
Who e'er keeps me, let my heart be his guard;
Thou canst not then use rigour in my gaol:
 And yet thou wilt; for I, being pent in thee,
 Perforce am thine, and all that is in me.

CXXXIV

So, now I have confess'd that he is thine,
And I myself am mortgag'd to thy will,
Myself I'll forfeit, so that other mine
Thou wilt restore, to be my comfort still:
But thou wilt not, nor he will not be free,
For thou art covetous, and he is kind;
He learn'd but, surety-like, to write for me,
Under that bond that him as fast doth bind.
The statue of thy beauty thou wilt take,
Thou usurer, that putt'st forth all to use,
And sue a friend came debtor for my sake;
So him I lose through my unkind abuse.
    Him have I lost; thou hast both him and me:
    He pays the whole, and yet am I not free.

CXXXV

Whoever hath her wish, thou hast thy *Will*,
And *Will* to boot, and *Will* in over-plus;
More than enough am I that vex thee still,
To thy sweet will making addition thus.
Wilt thou, whose will is large and spacious,
Not once vouchsafe to hide my will in thine?
Shall will in others seem right gracious,
And in my will no fair acceptance shine?
The sea, all water, yet receives rain still,
And, in abundance, addeth to his store;
So thou, being rich in *Will*, add to thy *Will*
One will of mine, to make thy large *Will* more.
    Let no unkind, no fair beseechers kill;
    Think all but one, and me in that one *Will*.

CXXXVI

If thy soul check thee that I come so near,
Swear to thy blind soul that I was thy *Will*,
And will, thy soul knows, is admitted there;
Thus far for love, my love-suit, sweet, fulfil.
Will will fulfil the treasure of thy love,
Ay, fill it full with wills, and my will one,
In things of great receipt with ease we prove
Among a number one is reckon'd none:
Then in the number let me pass untold,
Though in thy stores' account I one must be;
For nothing hold me, so it please thee hold
That nothing me, a something sweet to thee:
    Make but my name thy love, and love that still,
    And then thou lov'st me,—for my name is *Will*.

CXXXVII

Thou blind fool, Love, what dost thou to mine eyes,
That they behold, and see not what they see?
They know what beauty is, see where it lies,
Yet what the best is, take the worst to be.
If eyes, corrupt by over-partial looks,
Be anchor'd in the bay where all men ride,
Why of eyes' falsehood hast thou forged hooks,
Whereto the judgment of my heart is tied?
Why should my heart think that a several plot,
Which my heart knows the wide world's common place?
Or mine eyes, seeing this, say this is not,
To put fair truth upon so foul a face?
    In things right-true my heart and eyes have err'd,
    And to this false plague are they now transferr'd.

CXXXVIII

When my love swears that she is made of truth
I do believe her, though I know she lies,
That she might think me some untutor'd youth,
Unlearned in the world's false subtleties.
Thus vainly thinking that she thinks me young,
Although she knows my days are past the best,
Simply I credit her false-speaking tongue:
On both sides thus is simple truth supprest.
But wherefore says she not she is unjust?
And wherefore say not I that I am old?
O, love's best habit is in seeming trust,
And age in love loves not to have years told:
    Therefore I lie with her and she with me,
    And in our faults by lies we flatter'd be.

CXXXIX

O, call not me to justify the wrong
That thy unkindness lays upon my heart;
Wound me not with thine eye, but with thy tongue;
Use power with power, and slay me not by art.
Tell me thou lov'st elsewhere; but in my sight,
Dear heart, forbear to glance thine eye aside:
What need'st thou wound with cunning, when thy might
Is more than my o'erpress'd defence can 'bide?
Let me excuse thee: ah, my love well knows
Her pretty looks have been mine enemies!
And therefore from my face she turns my foes,
That they elsewhere might dart their injuries:
    Yet do not so; but since I am near slain,
    Kill me outright with looks, and rid my pain.

CXL

Be wise as thou art cruel; do not press
My tongue-tied patience with too much disdain;
Lest sorrow lend me words, and words express
The manner of my pity-wanting pain.
If I might teach thee wit, better it were,
Though not to love, yet, love, to tell me so;—
As testy sick men, when their deaths be near,
No news but health from their physicians know;—
For, if I should despair, I should grow mad,
And in my madness might speak ill of thee:
Now this ill-wresting world is grown so bad,
Mad slanderers by mad ears believed be.
    That I may not be so, nor thou belied,
    Bear thine eyes straight, though thy proud heart go wide.

CXLI

In faith, I do not love thee with mine eyes,
For they in thee a thousand errors note;
But 'tis my heart that loves what they despise,
Who, in despite of view, is pleas'd to dote;
Nor are mine ears with thy tongue's tune delighted;
Nor tender feeling, to base touches prone,
Nor taste, nor smell, desire to be invited
To any sensual feast with thee alone:
But my five wits nor my five senses can
Dissuade one foolish heart from serving thee,
Who leaves unsway'd the likeness of a man,
Thy proud heart's slave and vassal wretch to be:
    Only my plague thus far I count my gain,
    That she that makes me sin awards me pain.

CXLII

Love is my sin, and thy dear virtue hate,
Hate of my sin, grounded on sinful loving:
O, but with mine compare thou thine own state,
And thou shalt find it merits not reproving;
Or, if it do, not from those lips of thine,
That have profan'd their scarlet ornaments,
And seal'd false bonds of love as oft as mine;
Robb'd others' beds' revenues of their rents.
Be it lawful I love thee, as thou lov'st those
Whom thine eyes woo as mine importune thee:
Root pity in thy heart, that, when it grows,
Thy pity may deserve to pitied be.
 If thou dost seek to have what thou dost hide,
 By self-example mayst thou be denied!

CXLIII

Lo, as a careful housewife runs to catch
One of her feather'd creatures broke away,
Sets down her babe, and makes all swift despatch
In púrsuit of the thing she would have stay;
Whilst her neglected child holds her in chace,
Cries to catch her whose busy care is bent
To follow that which flies before her face,
Not prizing her poor infant's discontent;
So runn'st thou after that which flies from thee,
Whilst I thy babe chase thee afar behind;
But if thou catch thy hope, turn back to me,
And play the mother's part, kiss me, be kind:
 So will I pray that thou mayst have thy *Will*,
 If thou turn back, and my loud crying still.

CXLIV

Two loves I have of comfort and despair,
Which like two spirits do suggest me still;
The better angel is a man right fair,
The worser spirit a woman colour'd ill.
To win me soon to hell, my female evil
Tempteth my better angel from my side,
And would corrupt my saint to be a devil,
Wooing his purity with her foul pride.
And whether that my angel be turn'd fiend,
Suspect I may, yet not directly tell;
But being both from me, both to each friend,
I guess one angel in another's hell:
    Yet this shall I ne'er know, but live in doubt,
    Till my bad angel fire my good one out.

CXLV

Those lips that Love's own hand did make
Breath'd forth the sound that said, "I hate,"
To me that languish'd for her sake:
But when she saw my woeful state,
Straight in her heart did mercy come,
Chiding that tongue, that ever sweet
Was us'd in giving gentle doom;
And taught it thus anew to greet;
"I hate," she alter'd with an end,
That follow'd it as gentle day
Doth follow night, who, like a fiend,
From heaven to hell is flown away;
    "I hate," from hate away she threw,
    And sav'd my life, saying—"not you."

CXLVI

Poor soul, the centre of my sinful earth,
Fool'd by these rebel powers that thee array,
Why dost thou pine within and suffer dearth,
Painting thy outward walls so costly gay?
Why so large cost, having so short a lease,
Dost thou upon thy fading mansion spend?
Shall worms, inheritors of this excess,
Eat up thy charge? is this thy body's end?
Then, soul, live thou upon thy servant's loss,
And let that pine to aggravate thy store;
Buy terms divine in selling hours of dross;
Within be fed, without be rich no more:
　　So shalt thou feed on Death, that feeds on men,
　　And Death once dead, there's no more dying then.

CXLVII

My love is as a fever, longing still
For that which longer nurseth the disease;
Feeding on that which doth preserve the ill,
Th' uncertain-sickly appetite to please.
My reason, the physician to my love,
Angry that his prescriptions are not kept,
Hath left me, and I, desperate now, approve
Desire is death, which physic did except.
Past cure I am, now reason is past care,
And frantic-mad with evermore unrest;
My thoughts and my discourse as madmen's are,
At random from the truth vainly express'd;
　　For I have sworn thee fair, and thought thee bright,
　　Who art as black as hell, as dark as night.

CXLVIII

O me, what eyes hath Love put in my head,
Which have no correspondence with true sight!
Or, if they have, where is my judgment fled,
That censures falsely what they see aright?
If that be fair whereon my false eyes dote,
What means the world to say it is not so?
If it be not, then love doth well denote
Love's eye is not so true as all men's: no;
How can it? O, how can Love's eye be true,
That is so vex'd with watching and with tears?
No marvel, then, though I mistake my view;
The sun itself sees not, till heaven clears.
    O, cunning love! with tears thou keep'st me blind,
    Lest eyes well-seeing thy foul faults should find.

CXLIX

Canst thou, O cruel! say I love thee not,
When I, against myself, with thee partake?
Do I not think on thee, when I forgot
Am of myself, all tyrant, for thy sake?
Who hateth thee that I do call my friend?
On whom frown'st thou that I do fawn upon?
Nay if thou low'rst on me, do I not spend
Revenge upon myself with present moan?
What merit do I in myself respect,
That is so proud thy service to despise,
When all my best doth worship thy defect,
Commanded by the motion of thine eyes?
    But, love, hate on, for now I know thy mind;
    Those that can see thou lov'st, and I am blind.

CL

O, from what power hast thou this powerful might,
With insufficiency my heart to sway?
To make me give the lie to my true sight,
And swear that brightness doth not grace the day?
Whence hast thou this becoming of things ill,
That in the very refuse of thy deeds
There is such strength and warrantise of skill,
That, in my mind, thy worst all best exceeds?
Who taught thee how to make me love thee more,
The more I hear and see just cause of hate?
O, though I love what others do abhor,
With others thou shouldst not abhor my state:
    If thy unworthiness rais'd love in me,
    More worthy I to be belov'd of thee.

CLI

Love is too young to know what conscience is;
Yet who knows not, conscience is born of love?
Then, gentle cheater, urge not my amiss,
Lest guilty of my faults thy sweet self prove:
For thou betraying me, I do betray
My nobler part to my gross body's treason;
My soul doth tell my body that he may
Triumph in love; flesh stays no farther reason;
But, rising at thy name, doth point out thee
As his triumphant prize. Proud of this pride,
He is contented thy poor drudge to be,
To stand in thy affairs, fall by thy side.
    No want of conscience hold it that I call
    Her "love" for whose dear love I rise and fall.

CLII

In loving thee thou know'st I am forsworn,
But thou art twice forsworn, to me love swearing;
In act thy bed-vow broke, and new faith torn,
In vowing new hate after new love bearing.
But why of two oaths' breach do I accuse thee,
When I break twenty? I am perjured most;
For all my vows are oaths but to misuse thee,
And all my honest faith in thee is lost:
For I have sworn deep oaths of thy deep kindness,
Oaths of thy love, thy truth, thy constancy;
And, to enlighten thee, gave eyes to blindness,
Or made them swear against the thing they see;
    For I have sworn thee fair,—more perjur'd I,
    To swear, against the truth, so foul a lie!

CLIII

Cupid laid by his brand, and fell asleep:
A maid of Dian's this advantage found,
And his love-kindling fire did quickly steep
In a cold valley-fountain of that ground;
Which borrow'd from this holy fire of Love
A dateless-lively heat, still to endure,
And grew a seething bath, which yet men prove
Against strange maladies a sovereign cure.
But at my mistress' eye Love's brand new-fir'd,
The boy for trial needs would touch my breast;
I, sick withal, the help of bath desir'd,
And thither hied, a sad distemper'd guest,
    But found no cure: the bath for my help lies
    Where Cupid got new fire,—my mistress' eyes.

CLIV

The little Love-god, lying once asleep,
Laid by his side his heart-inflaming brand,
Whilst many nymphs that vow'd chaste life to keep
Came tripping by; but in her maiden hand
The fairest votary took up that fire
Which many legions of true hearts had warm'd;
And so the general of hot desire
Was sleeping by a virgin hand disarm'd.
This brand she quenched in a cool well by,
Which from Love's fire took heat perpetual,
Growing a bath and healthful remedy
For men diseas'd; but I, my mistress' thrall,
  Came there for cure, and this by that I prove,
  Love's fire heats water, water cools not love.

Selected Verse
from the Plays

SELECTED VERSE
FROM THE PLAYS

TO SILVIA
from *Two Gentlemen of Verona*

My thoughts do harbour with my Silvia nightly;
    And slaves they are to me, that send them flying:
O, could their master come and go as lightly,
    Himself would lodge, where senseless they are lying.
My herald thoughts in thy pure bosom rest them;
    While I, their king, that thither them importune,
Do curse the grace that with such grace hath bless'd them,
    Because myself do want my servants' fortune:
I curse myself, for they are sent by me,
That they should harbour where their lord should be.
Silvia, this night I will enfranchise thee.

SONG OF SILVIA

from *Two Gentlemen of Verona*

Who is Silvia? what is she,
  That all our swains commend her?
Holy, fair, and wise is she,
  The heaven such grace did lend her,
That she might admired be.

Is she kind as she is fair?
  For beauty lives with kindness:
Love doth to her eyes repair,
  To help him of his blindness;
And, being help'd, inhabits there.

Then to Silvia let us sing,
  That Silvia is excelling;
She excels each mortal thing,
  Upon the dull earth dwelling:
To her let us garlands bring.

"SO SWEET A KISS"
from *Love's Labour's Lost*

So sweet a kiss the golden sun gives not
    To those fresh morning drops upon the rose,
As thy eye-beams, when their fresh rays have smot
    The dew of night that on my cheeks down flows:
Nor shines the silver moon one-half so bright
    Through the transparent bosom of the deep,
As doth thy face through tears of mine give light:
    Thou shin'st in every tear that I do weep;
No drop but as a coach doth carry thee,
    So ridest thou triumphing in my woe:
Do but behold the tears that swell in me,
    And they thy glory through my grief will show:
But do not love thyself; then thou wilt keep
My tears for glasses, and still make me weep.
O queen of queens, how far dost thou excel!
No thought can think, nor tongue of mortal tell.—

SPRING AND WINTER
from *Love's Labour's Lost*

I

SPRING. When daisies pied, and violets blue,
And lady-smocks all silver white,
And cuckoo-buds of yellow hue,
Do paint the meadows with delight,
The cuckoo then, on every tree,
Mocks married men, for thus sings he,
Cuckoo;
Cuckoo, cuckoo,—O word of fear,
Unpleasing to a married ear!

II

When shepherds pipe on oaten straws,
And merry larks are ploughmen's clocks,
When turtles tread, and rooks, and daws,
And maidens bleach their summer-smocks,
The cuckoo then, on every tree,
Mocks married men, for thus sings he,
Cuckoo;
Cuckoo, cuckoo,—O word of fear,
Unpleasing to a married ear!

III

WINTER. When icicles hang by the wall,
And Dick the shepherd blows his nail,
And Tom bears logs into the hall,
And milk comes frozen home in pail,

When blood is nipp'd, and ways be foul,
Then nightly sings the staring owl,
    To-who;
Tu-whit, to-who, a merry note,
While greasy Joan doth keel the pot.

IV

When all aloud the wind doth blow,
    And coughing drowns the parson's saw,
And birds sit brooding in the snow,
    And Marian's nose looks red and raw;
When roasted crabs hiss in the bowl,
Then nightly sings the staring owl,
    To-who;
Tu-whit, to-who, a merry note,
While greasy Joan doth keel the pot.

"EXAMINE EVERY MARRIED LINEAMENT"
from *Romeo and Juliet*

Examine every married lineament,
And see how one another lends content;
And what obscur'd in this fair volume lies,
Find written in the margent of his eyes.
This precious book of love, this unbound lover,
To beautify him, only lacks a cover:
The fish lives in the sea; and 'tis much pride,
For fair without, the fair within to hide:
That book in many's eyes doth share the glory,
That in gold clasps locks in the golden story;
So shall you share all that he doth possess,
By having him, making yourself no less.

QUEEN MAB

from *Romeo and Juliet*

She is the fairies' midwife; and she comes
In shape no bigger than an agate-stone
On the fore-finger of an alderman,
Drawn with a team of little atomies
Athwart men's noses as they lie asleep:
Her waggon-spokes made of long spinners' legs;
The cover, of the wings of grasshoppers;
Her traces, of the smallest spider's web;
Her collars, of the moonshine's wat'ry beams:
Her whip, of cricket's bone; the lash, of film:
Her waggoner, a small grey-coated gnat,
Not half so big as a round little worm
Prick'd from the lazy finger of a maid:
Her chariot is an empty hazel-nut,
Made by the joiner squirrel, or old grub,
Time out o' mind the fairies' coach-makers.
And in this state she gallops night by night
Through lovers' brains, and then they dream of love:
On courtiers' knees, that dream on court'sies straight:
O'er lawyers' fingers, who straight dream on fees:
O'er ladies' lips, who straight on kisses dream;
Which oft the angry Mab with blisters plagues,
Because their breaths with sweet-meats tainted are.
Sometime she gallops o'er a courtier's nose,
And then dreams he of smelling out a suit:
And sometime comes she with a tithe-pig's tail,
Tickling a parson's nose as 'a lies asleep,
Then dreams he of another benefice:

Sometime she driveth o'er a soldier's neck,
And then dreams he of cutting foreign throats,
Of breaches, ambuscadoes, Spanish blades,
Of healths five fathom deep; and then anon
Drums in his ear; at which he starts, and wakes;
And, being thus frighted, swears a prayer or two,
And sleeps again. This is that very Mab,
That plats the manes of horses in the night;
And bakes the elf-locks in foul sluttish hairs,
Which, once untangled, much misfortune bodes.
This is the hag, when maids lie on their backs,
That presses them, and learns them first to bear,
Making them women of good carriage.
This is she.

CHORUS

from *Romeo and Juliet*

Now old desire doth in his death-bed lie,
    And young affection gapes to be his heir;
That fair, for which love groan'd for, and would die,
    With tender Juliet match'd, is now not fair.
Now Romeo is belov'd, and loves again,
    Alike bewitched by the charm of looks;
But to his foe suppos'd he must complain,
    And she steal love's sweet bait from fearful hooks:
Being held a foe, he may not have access
    To breathe such vows as lovers use to swear;
And she as much in love, her means much less,
    To meet her new-beloved any where:
But passion lends them power, time means to meet,
Temp'ring extremities with extreme sweet.

"THE GREY-EY'D MORN SMILES ON THE FROWNING NIGHT"

from *Romeo and Juliet*

The grey-ey'd morn smiles on the frowning night,
Checkering the eastern clouds with streaks of light;
And flecked darkness like a drunkard reels
From forth day's path, and Titan's fiery wheels:
Now ere the sun advance his burning eye,
The day to cheer, and night's dank dew to dry,
I must up-fill this osier cage of ours,
With baleful weeds, and precious-juiced flowers.
The earth, that's nature's mother, is her tomb;
What is her burying grave, that is her womb:
And from her womb children of divers kind,
We sucking on her natural bosom find;
Many for many virtues excellent,
None but for some, and yet all different.
O, mickle is the powerful grace, that lies
In plants, herbs, stones, and their true qualities:
For nought so vile that on the earth doth live,
But to the earth some special good doth give;
Nor aught so good, but, strain'd from that fair use,
Revolts from true birth, stumbling on abuse:
Virtue itself turns vice, being misapplied;

And vice sometime 's by action dignified.
Within the infant rind of this weak flower
Poison hath residence, and medicine power:
For this, being smelt, with that part cheers each part;
Being tasted, slays all senses with the heart.
Two such opposed kings encamp them still
In man as well as herbs,—grace, and rude will;
And, where the worser is predominant,
Full soon the canker death eats up that plant.

"OVER HILL, OVER DALE"
from *Midsummer Night's Dream*

Over hill, over dale,
    Thorough bush, thorough brier,
Over park, over pale,
    Thorough flood, thorough fire,
I do wander everywhere,
Swifter than the moon's sphere;
And I serve the fairy queen,
To dew her orbs upon the green:
The cowslips tall her pensioners be;
In their gold coats spots you see;
Those be rubies, fairy favours,
In those freckles live their savours.

"I KNOW A BANK"
from *Midsummer Night's Dream*

I know a bank where the wild thyme blows,
Where ox-lips and the nodding violet grows;
Quite over-canopied with luscious woodbine,
With sweet musk-roses, and with eglantine:
There sleeps Titania, sometime of the night,
Lull'd in these flowers with dances and delight;
And there the snake throws her enamell'd skin,
Weed wide enough to wrap a fairy in.

LULLABY
from *Midsummer Night's Dream*

1 FAIRY. You spotted snakes, with double tongue,
         Thorny hedgehogs, be not seen;
    Newts, and blind-worms, do no wrong;
      Come not near our fairy queen:

CHORUS.   Philomel, with melody
        Sing in our sweet lullaby;
   Lulla, lulla, lullaby; lulla, lulla, lullaby;
      Never harm, nor spell nor charm,
      Come our lovely lady nigh;
      So, good night, with lullaby.

2 FAIRY. Weaving spiders, come not here:
      Hence, you long-legg'd spinners, hence:
   Beetles black, approach not near;
      Worm, nor snail, do no offence.

"THE OOSEL-COCK"

from *Midsummer Night's Dream*

The oosel-cock, so black of hue,
    With orange-tawny bill,
The throstle with his note so true,
    The wren with little quill;
The finch, the sparrow, and the lark,
    The plain-song cuckoo gray,
Whose note full many a man doth mark,
    And dares not answer, nay—

"ALL THAT GLISTERS"

from *The Merchant of Venice*

All that glisters is not gold,
Often have you heard that told:
Many a man his life hath sold,
But my outside to behold:
Gilded tombs do worms infold.
Had you been as wise as bold,
Young in limbs, in judgment old,
Your answer had not been inscroll'd:
Fare you well; your suit is cold.

"THE FIRE SEVEN TIMES TRIED THIS"
from *The Merchant of Venice*

The fire seven times tried this;
Seven times tried that judgment is,
That did never choose amiss:
Some there be that shadows kiss,
Such have but a shadow's bliss:
There be fools alive, I wis,
Silver'd o'er; and so was this.
Take what wife you will to bed,
I will ever be your head:
So begone: you are sped.

THE CASKET
from *The Merchant of Venice*

Tell me where is fancy bred,
Or in the heart, or in the head?
How begot, how nourished?
    Reply, reply.

It is engender'd in the eyes,
With gazing fed; and fancy dies
In the cradle where it lies;
Let us all ring fancy's knell;
I'll begin it,—Ding, dong, bell.
    Ding, dong, bell.

FORTUNE

from *The Merchant of Venice*

You that choose not by the view,
Chance as fair, and choose as true!
Since this fortune falls to you,
Be content, and seek no new.
If you be well pleas'd with this,
And hold your fortune for your bliss,
Turn you where your lady is,
And claim her with a loving kiss.

"LOVE LIKE A SHADOW FLIES"

from *The Merry Wives of Windsor*

Love like a shadow flies,
When substance love pursues;
Pursuing that that flies,
And flying what pursues.

"FIE ON SINFUL FANTASY!"
from *The Merry Wives of Windsor*

Fie on sinful fantasy!
Fie on lust and luxury!
Lust is but a bloody fire,
Kindled with unchaste desire,
Fed in heart, whose flames aspire,
As thoughts do blow them, higher and higher.
    Pinch him, fairies, mutually;
    Pinch him for his villainy;
Pinch him, and burn him, and turn him about,
Till candles, and star-light, and moonshine be out.

"HEY NONNY, NONNY"
from *Much Ado About Nothing*

I

Sigh no more, ladies, sigh no more,
    Men were deceivers ever;
One foot in sea, and one on shore,
    To one thing constant never:
        Then sigh not so,
        But let them go,
    And be you blithe and bonny;
Converting all your sounds of woe
    Into, Hey nonny, nonny.

II

Sing no more ditties, sing no mo,
　　Of dumps so dull and heavy;
The fraud of men was ever so,
　　Since summer first was leafy.
　　　　Then sigh not so,
　　　　But let them go,
　　　　And be you blithe and bonny;
Converting all your sounds of woe
　　Into, Hey nonny, nonny.

EPITAPH

from *Much Ado About Nothing*

Done to death by slanderous tongues
　　Was the Hero that here lies:
Death, in guerdon of her wrongs,
　　Gives her fame which never dies:
So the life, that died with shame,
Lives in death with glorious fame.

"PARDON, GODDESS OF THE NIGHT"
from *Much Ado About Nothing*

Pardon, goddess of the night,
Those that slew thy virgin knight;
For the which, with songs of woe,
Round about her tomb they go.
Midnight, assist our moan,
Help us to sigh and groan,
    Heavily, heavily:
Graves yawn and yield your dead,
Till death be uttered,
    Heavenly, heavenly.

A TRUTH
from *All's Well That Ends Well*

For I the ballad will repeat,
    Which men full true shall find;
Your marriage comes by destiny,
    Your cuckoo sings by kind.

ONE GOOD IN TEN
from *All's Well That Ends Well*

Was this fair face the cause, quoth she,
    Why the Grecians sacked Troy?
Fond done, done fond,
    Was this king Priam's joy.
With that she sighed as she stood,
With that she sighed as she stood.
    And gave this sentence then;
Among nine bad if one be good,
Among nine bad if one be good,
    There's yet one good in ten.

"I AM ST. JAQUES' PILGRIM"
from *All's Well That Ends Well*

I am St. Jaques' pilgrim, thither gone:
    Ambitious love hath so in me offended,
That bare-foot plod I the cold ground upon,
    With sainted vow my faults to have amended.
Write, write, that, from the bloody course of war,
    My dearest master, your dear son, may hie;
Bless him at home in peace, whilst I from far,
His name with zealous fervour sanctify:
His taken labours bid him me forgive;
    I, his despiteful Juno, sent him forth
From courtly friends, with camping foes to live,
    Where death and danger dog the heels of worth:
He is too good and fair for death and me;
Whom I myself embrace, to set him free.

"UNDER THE GREENWOOD TREE"
from *As You Like It*

Under the greenwood tree,
Who loves to lie with me,
And turn his merry note
Unto the sweet bird's throat,
Come hither, come hither, come hither;
Here shall he see
No enemy,
But winter and rough weather.

Who doth ambition shun,
And loves to live i' the sun,
Seeking the food he eats,
And pleas'd with what he gets,
Come hither, come hither, come hither;
Here shall he see
No enemy,
But winter and rough weather.

"ALL THE WORLD'S A STAGE"
from *As You Like It*

All the world's a stage,
And all the men and women merely players:
They have their exits and their entrances,
And one man in his time plays many parts,
His acts being seven ages. At first the infant,
Mewling and puking in the nurse's arms:
Then the whining school-boy, with his satchel
And shining morning-face, creeping like snail
Unwillingly to school. And then the lover,
Sighing like furnace, with a woeful ballad
Made to his mistress' eyebrow. Then a soldier,
Full of strange oaths, and bearded like the pard,
Jealous in honour, sudden, and quick in quarrel,
Seeking the bubble reputation,
Even in the cannon's mouth. And then the justice,
In fair round belly with good capon lin'd,
With eyes severe and beard of formal cut,
Full of wise saws and modern instances;
And so he plays his part. The sixth age shifts
Into the lean and slipper'd pantaloon,
With spectacles on nose and pouch on side;
His youthful hose, well sav'd, a world too wide
For his shrunk shank; and his big manly voice,
Turning again toward childish treble, pipes
And whistles in his sound. Last scene of all,
That ends this strange eventful history,
Is second childishness, and mere oblivion,
Sans teeth, sans eyes, sans taste, sans everything.

"BLOW, BLOW, THOU WINTER WIND"
from *As You Like It*

Blow, blow, thou winter wind,
Thou art not so unkind
    As man's ingratitude;
Thy tooth is not so keen
Because thou art not seen,
    Although thy breath be rude.
Heigh-ho! sing, heigh-ho! unto the green holly;
Most friendship is feigning, most loving mere folly:
    Then, heigh-ho, the holly!
        This life is most jolly.

Freeze, freeze, thou bitter sky,
That dost not bite so nigh
    As benefits forgot:
Though thou the waters warp,
Thy sting is not so sharp
    As friend remember'd not.
Heigh-ho! sing, heigh-ho! unto the green holly;
Most friendship is feigning, most loving mere folly:
    Then, heigh-ho, the holly!
        This life is most jolly.

ROSALIND

from *As You Like It*

From the east to western Ind,
No jewel is like Rosalind.
Her worth, being mounted on the wind,
Through all the world bears Rosalind.
All the pictures fairest lin'd
Are but black to Rosalind.
Let no face be kept in mind,
But the fair of Rosalind.
If a hart do lack a hind,
Let him seek out Rosalind.
If the cat will after kind,
So, be sure, will Rosalind.
Winter garments must be lin'd,
So must slender Rosalind.
They that reap must sheaf and bind,
Then to cart with Rosalind.
Sweetest nut hath sourest rind,
Such a nut is Rosalind.
He that sweetest Rose will find,
Must find love's prick and Rosalind.

"WHY SHOULD THIS A DESERT BE?"
from *As You Like It*

Why should this a desert be?
    For it is unpeopled? No;
Tongues I'll hang on every tree,
    That shall civil sayings show.
Some, how brief the life of man
    Runs his erring pilgrimage;
That the stretching of a span
    Buckles in his sum of age.
Some, of violated vows
    'Twixt the souls of friend and friend:
But upon the fairest boughs,
    Or at every sentence' end,
Will I Rosalinda write;
    Teaching all that read, to know
The quintessence of every sprite
    Heaven would in little show.
Therefore heaven nature charg'd
    That one body should be fill'd
With all graces wide enlarg'd:
    Nature presently distill'd
Helen's cheek, but not her heart;
    Cleopatra's majesty,
Atalanta's better part,
    Sad Lucretia's modesty.
Thus Rosalind of many parts
    By heavenly synod was devis'd,
Of many faces, eyes, and hearts,
    To have the touches dearest priz'd.
Heaven would that she these gifts should have,
    And I to live and die her slave.

"ART THOU GOD TO
SHEPHERD TURN'D"
from *As You Like It*

Art thou god to shepherd turn'd,
That a maiden's heart hath burn'd?—
Why, thy godhead laid apart,
Warr'st thou with a woman's heart?
Whiles the eyes of man did woo me,
That could do no vengeance to me.—
If the scorn of your bright eyne
Have power to raise such love in mine,
Alack, in me what strange effect
Would they work in mild aspéct!
Whiles you chid me, I did love,
How then might your prayers move!
He that brings this love to thee,
Little knows this love in me:
And by him seal up thy mind,
Whether that thy youth and kind
Will the faithful offer take
Of me, and all that I can make;
Or else by him my love deny,
And then I'll study how to die.

INSCRIPTION ON MARINA'S MONUMENT

from *Pericles*

The fairest, sweet'st, and best lies here,
Who wither'd in her spring of year:
She was of Tyrus the king's daughter,
On whom foul death hath made this slaughter;
Marina was she call'd; and at her birth,
Thetis, being proud, swallow'd some part o' the earth:
Therefore the earth, fearing to be o'erflow'd,
Hath Thetis' birth-child on the heavens bestow'd;
Wherefore she does, and swears she'll never stint,
Make raging battery upon shores of flint.

O MISTRESS MINE

from *Twelfth Night; Or, What You Will*

O mistress mine, where are you roaming?
O, stay and hear; your true-love's coming,
　　That can sing both high and low:
Trip no further, pretty sweeting;
Journeys end in lovers' meeting,
　　Every wise man's son doth know.
What is love? 'tis not hereafter;
Present mirth hath present laughter;
　　What's to come is still unsure:
In delay there lies no plenty;
Then come kiss me, sweet-and-twenty:
　　Youth's a stuff will not endure.

"COME AWAY, COME AWAY, DEATH"
from *Twelfth Night; Or, What You Will*

Come away, come away, death,
And in sad cypress let me be laid;
    Fly away, fly breath;
I am slain by a fair cruel maid.
    My shroud of white, stuck all with yew,
        O, prepare it!
    My part of death, no one so true
        Did share it.

Not a flower, not a flower sweet,
On my black coffin let there be strown;
    Not a friend, not a friend greet
My poor corpse, where my bones shall be thrown:
    A thousand thousand sighs to save,
        Lay me, O, where
    Sad true lover ne'er find my grave,
        To weep there!

THE CLOSING SONG

from *Twelfth Night; Or, What You Will*

When that I was and a little tiny boy,
    With hey, ho, the wind and the rain:
A foolish thing was but a toy,
    For the rain it raineth every day.

But when I came to man's estate,
    With hey, ho, the wind and the rain:
'Gainst knaves and thieves men shut their gate,
    For the rain it raineth every day.

But when I came, alas! to wive,
    With hey, ho, the wind and the rain:
By swaggering could I never thrive,
    For the rain it raineth every day.

But when I came unto my beds,
    With hey, ho, the wind and the rain:
With toss-pots still had drunken heads,
    For the rain it raineth every day.

A great while ago the world begun,
    With hey, ho, the wind and the rain:
But that's all one, our play is done,
    And we'll strive to please you every day.

APEMANTUS' GRACE
from *Timon of Athens*

Immortal gods, I crave no pelf;
I pray for no man but myself:
Grant I may never prove so fond,
To trust man on his oath or bond;
Or a harlot, for her weeping;
Or a dog, that seems a-sleeping;
Or a keeper with my freedom;
Or my friends, if I should need 'em.
Amen. So fall to 't:
Rich men sin, and I eat root.

SONG
from *Measure for Measure*

Take, O, take those lips away,
    That so sweetly were forsworn;
And those eyes, the break of day,
    Lights that do mislead the morn:
But my kisses bring again,
                        bring again,
Seals of love, but seal'd in vain,
                seal'd in vain.

"ORPHEUS, WITH HIS LUTE, MADE TREES"

from *King Henry the Eighth*

Orpheus, with his lute, made trees,
And the mountain-tops that freeze,
  Bow themselves, when he did sing:
To his music, plants and flowers
Ever sprung; as sun and showers
  There had made a lasting spring.
Every thing that heard him play,
Even the billows of the sea,
  Hung their heads, and then lay by.
In sweet music is such art;
Killing care and grief of heart,
  Fall asleep, or, hearing, die.

ARISE

from *Cymbeline*

Hark! hark! the lark at heaven's gate sings,
  And Phoebus 'gins arise,
His steeds to water at those springs
  On chalic'd flowers that lies;
And winking Mary-buds begin
  To ope their golden eyes;
With everything that pretty is,
  My lady sweet, arise:
    Arise, arise.

"HE, WHO THE SWORD OF HEAVEN WILL BEAR"

from *Measure for Measure*

He, who the sword of heaven will bear,
Should be as holy as severe;
Pattern in himself to know,
Grace to stand, and virtue go;
More nor less to others paying,
Than by self offences weighing.
Shame to him whose cruel striking
Kills for faults of his own liking!
Twice treble shame on Angelo,
To weed my vice and let his grow!
O, what may man within him hide,
Though angel on the outward side!
How may likeness, made in crimes,
Making practice on the times,
To draw with idle spiders' strings
Most pond'rous and substantial things!
Craft against vice I must apply:
With Angelo to-night shall lie
His old betrothed but despis'd;
So disguise shall, by the disguis'd,
Pay with falsehood false exacting,
And perform an old contracting.

"FEAR NO MORE THE HEAT
O' THE SUN"
from *Cymbeline*

Fear no more the heat o' the sun,
 Nor the furious winter's rages;
Thou thy worldly task hast done,
 Home art gone, and ta'en thy wages:
Golden lads and girls all must,
As chimney-sweepers, come to dust.

Fear no more the frown o' the great,
 Thou art past the tyrant's stroke;
Care no more to clothe and eat;
 To thee the reed is as the oak:
The sceptre, learning, physic, must
All follow this, and come to dust.

Fear no more the light'ning flash,
 Nor the all-dreaded thunder-stone;
Fear not slander, censure rash;
 Thou hast finish'd joy and moan:
All lovers young, all lovers must
Consign to thee, and come to dust.

SLEEP

from *The Tempest*

While you here do snoring lie,
Open-eyed Conspiracy
　　His time doth take:
If of life you keep a care,
Shake off slumber, and beware.
　　Awake! awake!

A SCURVY TUNE

from *The Tempest*

The master, the swabber, the boatswain, and I,
　　The gunner, and his mate,
Lov'd Mall, Meg, and Marian, and Margery,
　　But none of us car'd for Kate:
　　For she had a tongue with a tang,
　　Would cry to a sailor, "Go hang:"
She lov'd not the savour of tar nor of pitch,
Yet a tailor might scratch her where'er she did itch;
　　Then to sea, boys, and let her go hang!

ARIEL'S SONG

from *The Tempest*

Come unto these yellow sands,
  And then take hands:
Court'sied when you have and kiss'd,—
  The wild waves whist,—
Foot it featly here and there;
  And, sweet sprites, the burden bear.
  Hark, hark!
  Bowgh, wowgh.
The watch-dogs bark:
  Bowgh, wowgh.
Hark, hark! I hear
The strain of strutting chanticleer
Cry, cock-a-doodle-doo.

"FULL FATHOM FIVE THY FATHER LIES"

from *The Tempest*

Full fathom five thy father lies;
  Of his bones are coral made;
Those are pearls that were his eyes:
  Nothing of him that doth fade,
But doth suffer a sea-change
Into something rich and strange.
Sea-nymphs hourly ring his knell:
Hark! now I hear them,—Ding-dong, bell.

"WHERE THE BEE SUCKS"
from *The Tempest*

Where the bee sucks, there suck I;
In a cowslip's bell I lie,
There I couch when owls do cry:
On the bat's back I do fly
After summer merrily:
Merrily, merrily, shall I live now,
Under the blossom that hangs on the bough.

PROPHECY
from *King Lear*

When priests are more in word than matter;
When brewers mar their malt with water;
When nobles are their tailors' tutors;
No heretics burn'd, but wenches' suitors:
When every case in law is right;
No squire in debt, nor no poor knight;
When slanders do not live in tongues;
Nor cutpurses come not to throngs;
When usurers tell their gold i' the field;
And bawds and whores do churches build;—
Then shall the realm of Albion
Come to great confusion:
Then comes the time, who lives to see 't,
That going shall be us'd with feet.

"WHEN DAFFODILS BEGIN TO PEER"
from *Winter's Tale*

When daffodils begin to peer,—
    With hey! the doxy over the dale,—
Why then comes in the sweet o' the year;
    For the red blood reigns in the winter's pale.
The white sheet bleaching on the hedge,
    With hey! the sweet birds, O, how they sing!
Doth set my pugging tooth on edge;
    For a quart of ale is a dish for a king.

The lark that tirra-lirra chants,—
    With hey! with hey! the thrush and the jay,—
Are summer songs for me and my aunts,
    While we lie tumbling in the hay.
But shall I go mourn for that, my dear?
    The pale moon shines by night;
And when I wander here and there,
    I then do most go right.

If tinkers may have leave to live,
    And bear the sow-skin budget;
Then my account I well may give,
    And in the stocks avouch it.

"LAWN AS WHITE AS DRIVEN SNOW"
from *Winter's Tale*

Lawn as white as driven snow;
Cyprus black as e'er was crow;
Gloves as sweet as damask roses;
Masks for faces and for noses;
Bugle-bracelet, necklace-amber,
Perfume for a lady's chamber;
Golden quoifs and stomachers,
For my lads to give their dears;
Pins and poking-sticks of steel;
What maids lack from head to heel:
Come, buy of me, come; come buy, come buy;
Buy, lads, or else your lasses cry: come, buy.

"TO BE OR NOT TO BE"
from *Hamlet*

To be, or not to be,—that is the question:—
Whether 'tis nobler in the mind, to suffer
The slings and arrows of outrageous fortune,
Or to take arms against a sea of troubles,
And by opposing end them?—To die, to sleep,—
No more; and by a sleep to say we end
The heart-ache, and the thousand natural shocks
That flesh is heir to?—'tis a consummation
Devoutly to be wish'd. To die, to sleep;—
To sleep, perchance, to dream;—ay, there's the rub;
For in that sleep of death what dreams may come,
When we have shuffled off this mortal coil,
Must give us pause: there's the respect
That makes calamity of so long life;
For who would bear the whips and scorns of time,
The oppressor's wrong, the proud man's contumely,
The pangs of dispriz'd love, the law's delay,
The insolence of office, and the spurns
That patient merit of the unworthy takes,
When he himself might his quietus make
With a bare bodkin? who would fardels bear,

To grunt and sweat under a weary life,
But that the dread of something after death,—
The undiscover'd country, from whose bourn
No traveller returns,—puzzles the will,
And makes us rather bear those ills we have,
Than fly to others that we know not of?
Thus conscience does make cowards of us all;
And thus the native hue of resolution
Is sicklied o'er with the pale cast of thought;
And enterprises of great pith and moment,
With this regard, their currents turn awry,
And lose the name of action.

"THERE IS A TIDE"

from *Julius Caesar*

There is a tide in the affairs of men,
Which, taken at the flood, leads on to fortune;
Omitted, all the voyage of their life
Is bound in shallows and in miseries.
On such a full sea are we now afloat;
And we must take the current when it serves,
Or lose our ventures.

THE THREE WITCHES
from *Macbeth*

1 WITCH. Round about the caldron go;
In the poison'd entrails throw.—
Toad, that under cold stone,
Days and nights has thirty-one;
Swelter'd venom sleeping got,
Boil thou first i' the charmed pot!

ALL. Double, double toil and trouble;
Fire burn, and caldron bubble.

2 WITCH. Fillet of a fenny snake,
In the caldron boil and bake;
Eye of newt, and toe of frog,
Wool of bat, and tongue of dog,
Adder's fork, and blind-worm's sting,
Lizard's leg, and owlet's wing,—
For a charm of powerful trouble,
Like a hell-broth boil and bubble.

ALL. Double, double toil and trouble;
Fire burn, and caldron bubble.

3 WITCH. Scale of dragon; tooth of wolf;
Witches' mummy; maw and gulf
Of the ravin'd salt-sea shark;
Root of hemlock digg'd i' the dark;
Liver of blaspheming Jew;
Gall of goat, and slips of yew

Sliver'd in the moon's eclipse;
Nose of Turk, and Tartar's lips;
Finger of birth-strangled babe
Ditch-deliver'd by a drab,—
Make the gruel thick and slab:
Add thereto a tiger's chaudron,
For the ingredients of our caldron.

ALL.   Double, double toil and trouble;
Fire burn, and cauldron bubble.

2 WITCH. Cool it with a baboon's blood,
Then the charm is firm and good.

"WHEN REMEDIES ARE PAST"
from *Othello*

When remedies are past, the griefs are ended
By seeing the worst, which late on hopes depended.
To mourn a mischief that is past and gone
Is the next way to draw new mischief on.
What cannot be preserv'd, when Fortune takes,
Patience her injury a mockery makes.
The robb'd that smiles, steals something from the thief;
He robs himself that spends a bootless grief.